Great
Cycle Routes

Dorset and the New Forest

Jeremy Evans

Great Cycle Routes

Dorset and the New Forest

Jeremy Evans

The Crowood Press

First published in 1995 by
The Crowood Press Ltd
Ramsbury, Marlborough
Wiltshire SN8 2HR

British Library Cataloguing-in-Publication Data
A catalogue record for this book is available from the British Library.

ISBN 1 85223 851 8

Picture Credits
All photographs by Jeremy Evans
Line-drawings by Dave Ayres

Typeset by Creative Byte
Printed and bound by Redwood Books, Trowbridge

Contents

Introduction

RIDE INFORMATION

Area: Where the ride is located.

OS Map: The relevant OS Landranger 1:50 000 map for the route.

Route: Waymarks from start to finish, with OS grid reference numbers. All of the rides in this book bar the South Downs Way are circular, making it possible to start at a number of locations.

Nearest BR Stations: Most of the routes are accessible from a railway station. Owing to the market-led policies of British Rail which have become extremely bike-unfriendly, it is necessary to check restrictions and costs before you start and board a train.

Approx Length: In miles and kilometres. There should always be some allowance for getting lost or altering the route.

Time: This is very difficult to assess, and will depend on factors such as whether the tracks are dry, how many hills have to be climbed, how fast you ride, and how many pubs and places of interest there are en route.

Rating: An 'Easy' ride should be accessible for riders of all abilities, excluding sub-teenage children; a 'Moderate' ride may prove harder in terms of terrain, length, hills, churning those pedals, and possibly navigation; a 'Hard' ride is best suited to experienced offroad riders with a high level of commitment. However these ratings can be changed by the weather – for instance an 'Easy' ride in very dry weather may become a 'Hard' ride when the tracks are churned to mud.

Places to Visit / Top Pubs: Virtually all of these rides feature a number of possible pub stops. I have also indicated cafes and other facilities to enjoy along the route.

Stick to the rules, and you won't get into trouble!

COMMON SENSE OFFROAD

The tracks and trails used for offroad cycling must be shared. The basic problem for mountain bikers is that bikes are generally so much faster than walkers and horse-riders. That is the principal factor which causes antagonism, but why hurry? Why not take it easy and enjoy the ride? Stick to the following common sense rules, and everyone should be happy.

Be safe! Don't ride into danger.

1. Stay on public bridleways, byways or roads. Never ride on footpaths. Cycling on private tracks or open ground is not usually allowed without permission from the land owner. Always moderate your speed.

2. When you ride offroad, the bridleways and byways are classified as 'Highways'. This means the Highway Code applies, and you can be prosecuted for riding dangerously, especially if you are involved in an accident. Any form of racing is illegal on a public highway, unless it is a specially organized event and permission has been obtained. Byways may also be shared with motorized vehicles. They should give way to cyclists, but as when meeting any vehicle, it is necessary to play safe.

3. Learn how to prevent skids and ride with control to help prevent erosion, especially in the wet. If it is very wet, it is much better to push or carry your bike. Going off the official tracks and trails can cause unnecessary erosion, as well as damaging plant and animal environments.

4. When you meet other people offroad and in the countryside, be courteous and considerate. Always slow right down and give way to both walkers and horse-riders, even if it means dismounting and lifting your bike out of the way. Bikes are almost silent, so give warning of your approach in as polite a manner as possible. The British Horse Society would like you to 'Hail a Horse'; we think the very best policy is to come to a complete halt until the animals have passed you by. If you are riding in a group, all go to one side of the track. Take particular care when you ride past children – you may not worry them, but you may terrorize/infuriate their parents.

5. Make sure your bike is safe to ride, and won't let you down in the middle of nowhere on a fast downhill – learn basic maintenance and take essential spares. In the interests of safety take drink and food, and wear suitable clothing for the weather conditions and length of ride. It is wise to wear a helmet, putting a layer of polystyrene between your cranium and any hard object in the unlikely event of a bad fall particularly on-road.

6. To avoid getting lost, it is always wise to carry a compass and relevant map such as the OS 1:50, 000 Landranger series. You should know where you are, and have the ability to replan the route and cut the ride short.

7. Follow the Country Code. Leave nothing behind – no litter, no orange peel, the minimum of noise, no bad memories for yourself or for others, and if possible not even a sign of your wheeltracks. Always shut gates behind you (unless they should obviously be left open). Don't blast through fields of cows or sheep – neither they nor the farmer will like it. If you ride with a dog for a companion, be sure to keep it under control.

Ride together, but give way to walkers.

9

USE THAT MAP!

Unless the route is very easy or you know it well, you should never ride without a map, never ride without a compass. Once you get the hang of it, using them is easy and will ensure you know where you're heading.

A map is a diagram which shows the features of an area of land such as mountains, hills, woods, rivers, railways, roads, tracks, towns and buildings. All these and many other features are shown by special signs that map readers can understand. There is always a table on the map which explains the signs. On a 1:50, 000 map (OS Landranger) 1cm on the map equals 50,000cm on the ground; this equals 2cm for every kilometre, or 1 1/4 in per mile.

Do you know where you're going?

THE GRID SYSTEM: Maps are covered by a grid of numbered horizontal and vertical grid lines. The grid is used to find an exact place on a map. To find a grid reference position you read the first three numbers off the vertical grid line which is called the Eastings line. You then read the next three numbers off the horizontal Northings grid line. Where they meet is where you want to be.

CONTOURS: Contours are lines on a map which join areas that are the same height above sea level (in metres). The difference in height between the contour lines is called the vertical height. The closer the lines are the steeper the hill will be. Contour lines are spaced at 10m intervals on 1:50, 000 Landranger maps, and at 5m intervals on 1:25, 000 Outdoor Leisure maps.

It is generally best to arrange your ride so the climbs are short and steep and the descents are long and fast; it is also best to get major climbs out of the way early on the ride. Sometimes it is quite difficult to know if you will be going up or down; a river or stream on the map is a sure sign of dropping down to a valley, but you can also work it out by looking at the contour line height numbers, as the top of the number is always uphill.

USING A COMPASS: A compass is a valuable aid to finding your way. The most popular style is the Swedish-made Silva on which most modern hiking (equally suitable for biking) compasses are based. It is low in price, light, very tough, and easy to use.

The compass should be carried on a lanyard at all times; in bad visibility it may be the only means you have of finding the way. The compass needle always points to Magnetic North, but keep it away from close contact with any metallic object to which it might be sensitive. Knowing that the needle points North, you can always follow a course in the direction you wish to go. The vertical grid lines on a map point to Grid North; this may be a few degrees different from Magnetic North, but the difference is very small.

OFFROAD WITH KIDS

Why not take the kids with you? With a little care the whole family can have a great day out, and when the kids are too big for a child seat you can put them in the saddle and still stay in control.

There's no point in taking children cycling on-road or offroad if they don't enjoy it, because then you won't enjoy it. Always follow the three golden rules:

1. Make sure they're comfortable.

2. Keep them amused.

3. Don't bite off more than you can chew.

COMFORT: For a child up to around four years of age, go for the best rear-mounted child seat you can find. It must obviously be secure on the bike, with a high back and sides to help protect its occupant if you should fall, deep footwells to protect the feet, and a full harness to hold the child firmly in; a safety bar for the child to grip on to is also a worthwhile extra. Ideally, the seat should also be quick and easy to put on and take off your bike, so when you ride alone the seat doesn't have to go with you.

It's a good idea to get children used to wearing helmets as early as possible, but with very young children (under one year old) there is a often a problem making the helmet stay on. This results in a miserable baby with a helmet tipped down over its eyes; best then to do without the helmet and be extra careful, until you can be sure it will sit comfortably in position.

Make sure the straps of a helmet are sufficiently tight. Children won't like you fiddling under their chins, and your best policy is to train them to put on and take off the helmet themselves as young as possible, ensuring straps are adjusted to the right length. Shop around for a child helmet and do ask to try it on. As with most adult helmets, removable rubber pads are used to alter the internal diameter, but the most important consideration is that the design of the helmet and its straps hold it firmly on the head. Some helmets seem to want to slide forward on impact, which is useless.

The child is protected from the headwind by your body, but can still get pretty cold sitting there doing nothing; in winter, an all-in-one waterproof/windproof coverall suit does the job really well. Remember that young children require all sorts of extras – extra clothes, nappies, drink, apples, and so on. Try to keep their requirements down to an acceptable minimum; a neat solution is to carry extras in a small backpack that mounts behind the child seat itself.

A child seat can be a lot of fun.

KEEP THEM HAPPY: Young children generally love riding on the back of bikes, and want to tell you all about what's going on. It can be bad enough understanding them at the best of times, but in this situation it becomes ridiculous and your replies degenerate to a meaningless 'Yes' or 'No'.

With that level of conversation a child will only sit happily in its seat for so long; the duration will obviously be affected by the weather, especially if it's freezing and foul. Children like regular stops if they're to stay happy, so take a stash of little treats – apples, nuts and raisins, and so on – and ensure that you get to the picnic or pub (make sure they allow children) on time with the shortest part of the ride left for the end of the day.

Routes should be chosen with care and an eye on safety. A rock-strewn 'downhill extreme', which is just waiting to throw you over the handlebars, should obviously be avoided. To start with, keep to mellow and easy offroad routes such as those found in the New Forest or an old railway line such as the Downs Link in Sussex. Moderate uphills are all right when the weight of the child helps back wheel traction; immod-erate uphills are plain stupid, as you wheeze and groan pushing both bike and child together.

What about downhills? As long as you're in control there's no danger in going fast on a smooth track or road. Rather than hitting the brakes, it's better to treat it as a laugh and teach the child to get used to the thrill of safe speed.

There comes a time when children grow too big and bored for a conventional rear-mounted seat, but too young to ride their own bike and keep pace (and keep safe) with adults. One answer is the Trailerbike, a remarkable hybrid, which claims it will take children from four to ten years old with a maximum weight of 42kg (6.5 stone). It allows you to ride with your child; they get all the fun of riding their own bike, but you have total control over their speed, where they go, and ultimately their safety. They can also pedal as much or as little as they like. If they have the muscle and aptitude, they'll help push you uphill as well as down.

The Trailerbike is a hybrid which is excellent as children get older.

Abide by the rules – never ride on footpaths.

OFFROAD RIGHTS OF WAY IN ENGLAND & WALES

PUBLIC BRIDLEWAYS: Open to walkers and horse-riders, and also to cyclists since 1968. This right is not sacrosanct; bike bans are possible if riders are considered to have become too much of a nuisance.

PUBLIC BYWAYS: Usually unsurfaced tracks open to cyclists, walkers, horse-riders and vehicles which have right of access to houses.

PUBLIC FOOTPATHS: No rights to cycle. You probably have the right to push a bike, but the temptation to ride is high and it is best to avoid footpaths whenever possible.

FORESTRY COMMISSION: Access on designated cycle paths, or by permission from the local Forest Manager. At present there is a general presumption in favour of bikes using Forestry land gratis; this may change.

DESIGNATED CYCLE PATHS: Specially built cycle tracks for urban areas; or using Forestry Commission land or railway lines.

PAVEMENTS: Cycling is illegal on pavements. However it is frequently much safer and more pleasant than cycling on the road, and with the proviso that you take great care to avoid pedestrians (who are seldom seen on out-of-town pavements), using pavements can be perfectly reasonable.

WHAT IF BRIDLEWAYS AND BYWAYS ARE BLOCKED?

Cyclists are used to being on the defensive on Britain's roads; offroad they should stand up for their rights. The relevant landowner ánd local authority have the responsibility to maintain bridleways and byways and ensure they are passable with gates that work. It is illegal for a landowner to block a right of way, close or divert it (only the local authority or central government can do this), or put up a misleading notice to deter you from using it.

It is also illegal to plough up or disturb the surface of a right of way unless it is a footpath or bridleway running across a field. In that case the farmer must make good the surface within twenty-four hours or two weeks if it is the first disturbance for a particular crop. A bridleway so restored must have a minimum width of two metres, and its line must be clearly apparent on the ground. A farmer also has a duty to prevent any crops other than grass making a right of way difficult to follow. A bridleway across crops should have a two metre clear width; a field edge bridleway should have a clear width of three metres.

If you run into difficulty on any of the above, you can file a complaint with the Footpaths Officer at the local council, giving full details of the offence and a precise map reference of where it occurred.

Some bridleways are more difficult to follow than others!

OFFROAD CARE AND REPAIR

Have you decided on your route, got the right OS map, and your compass? Have you got all the right clothes – ready for rain, wind or sun – plus food and sufficient drink if it's going to be hot? That just leaves your bike, so don't risk getting let down by a breakdown.

Always prepare your bike carefully.

BRAKE CHECK: The most important part of your bike – if the brakes fail, you could be dead. Check the blocks for wear, turn them or change them as necessary. Lubricate the cables, check they won't slip, and if there is any sign of fraying, change them. Lube the brake pivots – if the spring return on the brakes isn't working well, they will need to be stripped down and cleaned.

WHEELS: Check your tyres for general wear and side-wall damage; look for thorns. If a wheel is out of line or dented, it needs to be adjusted with a spoke key; also check for loose spokes. Always carry a pump and a puncture repair kit.

CHAIN CARE: Give your chain a regular lube – there are all sorts of fancy spray lubes around, some of which cost a lot of money; however, although the more universal sorts are cheap and reliable, they do attract the dirt. If your chain and cogs are manky, clean them with a rag soaked in spray lubricant or a special 'chain bath'; adjust stiff links with a chain breaker, which is a useful tool to carry.

MOVING PARTS: Clean and lube the derailleur jockey wheels and gear cogs. Lube the freewheel with the bike on its side. Clean and lube the chainwheel gear mechanism. Lube and check the cables for both sets of gears. Lube the bottom bracket – the most basic method is to pour heavy oil down the top tube. Lube the pedals by taking off the end caps. Check that both the cranks and headset are tight. Check that the derailleur lines up properly.

Other things that may go wrong include breaking the chain or having a cable slip, though if you take care of your bike these occurrences are very rare. Just in case, however, it is wise to carry a chainlink extractor, which rejoins a broken chain, 4/5/6mm Allen keys, a small adjustable spanner, and a screwdriver with both a flat head and a Phillips head. The neat solution is a 'multi-tool' which includes all these items in one package.

PUNCTURE REPAIR

The most common offroad repair is a puncture and the most common cause is the hawthorn. To cope with this you need a pump, tyre levers and a puncture repair kit; you may also like to carry a spare tube. Always go for a full-size pump with the correct valve fitting; the pump should fit inside the frame, ideally on the down tube. A double-action pump puts in the air fastest.

Two tyre levers are sufficient, either in plastic or metal, whilst a spare tube saves the hassle of finding the leak and doing a patch offroad – unless you puncture twice.

1. Stop as soon as you feel a tyre go soggy: riding on a flat tyre is asking for trouble. Find a suitable place to do the repair – well away from any cars – and turn the bike upside-down. Take care you know where you put things down: it is too easy to lose that little black screw cap that covers the valve.

2. Undo the brake cable near the brake block, flip off the quick release lever at the hub, and remove the wheel. This is more of a fiddle with the back wheel, and it may be necessary to partly unscrew the hub.

3. You won't get the tube out unless it is well deflated. Carefully insert a lever to get the tyre wall off the rim, and then work the rim off all the way round one side using two levers.

4. Pull the tube out of the tyre. The next thing is to find the puncture. Inflate the tube, and then slowly pass it close to your ear and cheek. You should hear or feel the leak and be able to locate it. If this fails, you can try submerging the tube in a puddle and watch for tell-tale bubbles.

5. When you've found the puncture, keep a finger on it so you don't lose it. Roughen the surrounding area with the 'roughener' provided in your repair kit, and then cover the area with a patch-sized blob of glue. Now leave the glue to set for at least two minutes.

6. To find out what caused the puncture, run your fingers round the inside of the tyre; the probable cause is a thorn which is still in the tyre. Remove it carefully.

7. The glue should now be set enough to put on the patch which should bond straight to the tube. If it seems OK, partly inflate the tube, which makes things easier when getting the tyre back onto the rim.

8. Reassemble the wheel and put it back on the bike. Connecting the brake cable first ensures the wheel is centred by a pull on the brake lever before you tighten the quick release hub; it also ensures you don't ride off with the brake undone. Now inflate the tyre fully.

Mending the tube is usually a quick operation.

SAFETY OFFROAD

The first rule of offroad touring is to allow enough time. Getting caught by nightfall is foolhardy and potentially dangerous, particularly if the ride ends in an on-road section and you have no lights. So before you leave, work out how much time to allow, and be pessimistic. Your speed will depend on your skill, level of fitness, and the riding conditions.

Tackling a route after heavy rain in midwinter may take three times as long as the same route in dry summer weather. Riding along a disused railway line will be fast and easy; riding up and down big hills can be exceptionally demanding, and the difference in speed between a good and not so good rider will be much greater.

Don't 'race' unless it's official.

Riding in a group should ensure some degree of safety, but groups which are much bigger than three riders bring their own problems. They can put an unacceptable load on other people's enjoyment of the environment; walkers and horseriders were there first, and while they can cope with small groups of bike riders, it's no fun for them when a dozen or so Tour de France lookalikes blast through their favourite countryside. By contrast riding alone has much to recommend it; you cause minimum upset to others, and also don't have to worry about keeping up with the fastest member of the group, while the slowest rider doesn't have to worry about keeping up with you.

Whether you ride alone or in a small group, before leaving the golden rule is *tell someone:*

- When you're going.
- When you expect to be back.
- Give them some idea of your route.

It doesn't happen often, but riders do occasionally fall off and knock themselves out or break a few bones in the middle of nowhere; if that happened to you, it would be nice to know that someone would come looking for you, and that they'd be able to locate you before too long.

A First Aid kit is only of value if someone knows how to use it, and even then the constrictions of space and weight on a bike will make its application limited; some bandages and plasters will be enough to deal with minor cuts and abrasions, or possibly support a fracture. In most cases injuries from falls are fairly minor, and you can keep on riding; in more serious cases it will probably be a case of getting help ASAP, while caring for the injured rider:

- If two crash, help the worst injured first.
- If a rider is unconscious, don't leave him on his back. Use the First Aid 'recovery position' if you know how, and cover him with a coat if possible. If a rider is unconscious and not breathing, give the kiss of life if you know how.
- Staunch any bleeding by applying a pad or hand pressure; if bleeding is in an arm or leg, raise the injured limb unless broken.
- Don't move the rider if he seems to be paralysed, unless in immediate danger.
- Don't give the rider anything to eat, drink or smoke.
- Don't leave the injured rider alone.

If you ride regularly it's well worth attending a full length course to get a First Aid certificate which is valid for three years. These are run all round the UK by organizations such as the British Red Cross Society, whose phone number can be found in the local telephone directory.

Dorset Coastline and the Purbecks

The Dorset Coastline and the Purbeck Hills are a magnificent area of cliffs, coves and beaches stretching from Poole in the east to Lyme Regis on the Devon border in the west. While little of the long distance coastal footpath is open to cycles, there are many excellent bridleways and quiet country lanes that come close to the coast, offering splendid viewpoints for those who are willing to climb the hills. If you make the effort to get away from the crowds it's a wonderful area for both on-road and offroad cycling – just get out there and enjoy it.

Ride 1: Isle of Purbeck Circuit

Ride 2: Studland Heath

Ride 3: Arne Peninsula and Corfe Castle

Ride 4: Corfe and Kimmeridge Bay

Ride 5: Chaldon Down and Lulworth

Ride 6: The Hardy Monument

Ride 7: Abbotsbury to Litton Cheney

Ride 8: Litton Cheney and Bridport

Ride 9: Charmouth and Marshwood Vale

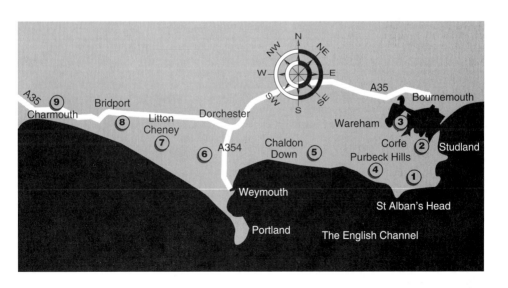

Isle of Purbeck Circuit

Offroad and On-Road

Area: The western end of the Purbecks between Swanage, Kimmeridge and Corfe Castle.

OS Map: Outdoor Leisure 15 – Purbeck; Landranger 195 – Bournemouth, Purbeck and surrounding area.

Route:
Corfe Castle (GR:960820)
Nine Barrow Down (GR:000813)
Studland (GR:037823)
Ballard Down (GR:034812)
Coombe (GR:008788)
Worth Matravers (973774)
Kingston (GR:957797)
Swyre Head (GR:934784)
Kimmeridge (GR:918801)
Steeple (GR:907810)
Church Knowle (GR:939818)
Corfe Castle (GR:960820)

Nearest BR Station: Wareham.

Approx Length: 35 miles (56km).

Time: Allow 5 hours.

Rating: Moderate. A fair number of hills, but nothing too dramatic and the riding surfaces are mainly good. 35 miles is a good distance and you'll know you've done it at the end.

This ride is a tour of the Isle of Purbeck and the Purbeck Hills along the coast from the seaside resort of Swanage, and if you're going to do just one ride in the area this is the one to go for. The route combines superb riding with great scenery, visits some of the main attractions of the area, and passes through easily ridden countryside with nice pubs along the way which should make it a very full day out.

1. From Corfe village centre follow the road downhill to the left, and then take the first right turning up a road going uphill beneath the old railway. Keep left by Challow Farm, going through the gate ahead and taking the bridleway that heads along the side of the hill, following a narrow track between stunted trees. There are two bridleways here leading all the way to the end of the down. One goes along the top and the other along the bottom, but the top route has the best views and is much more fun to ride.

2. Take the track that bears left up along the side of Challow Hill; it's steep in places but can be ridden all the way. It brings you to the top of Rollington Hill by an unmarked radio mast, and from there it's a straight ride for three miles or so along the top of Nine Barrow Down which is great offroad biking. At the end of the down, by the trig point at 654m, the track bears off to the right and then goes steeply down the side of Godlingston Hill by the Giant's Trencher.

3. At the bottom you're on the Studland-Swanage road. Turn left and immediately take the right fork for Studland, starting a steady uphill as the road bears round to the right. Ride straight on to Studland from here, and do a quick circuit of the village past the Bankes Arms Hotel, bearing right uphill to the farmyard from where a lane which is bridleway leads left up the hill.

4. Follow this lane uphill past an ugly patch of houses known as the Glebe. It gets quite steep, but is otherwise easy cycling until you get to the

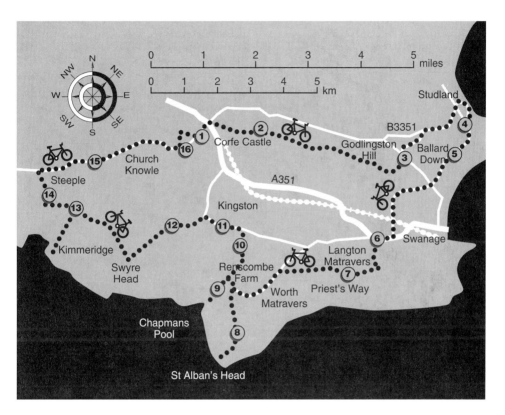

top of the Glebe, where the lane curves round to the right, and you bear off to the left through a gate on a track going up by the side of a National Trust sign. From here it is is a moderately steep and longish climb, eventually coming to the top of Ballard Down by a stone seat with the carved inscription 'Rest And Be Thankful'.

The views from here are excellent, looking out over the Bournemouth coastline and Poole Harbour to the north, with the Isle of Wight visible on a clear day due east, and the town of Swanage on the other side of the down.

5. Go through the gate and straight ahead, bearing right on the track that heads down the hillside towards Swanage. This gets fairly steep on a crumbly chalk surface which demands some careful riding, but otherwise is an enjoyable descent. Go through the gate at the bottom, fol-

lowing the sunken track out to a lane by Whitecliff Farm where you bear right and join the road on the outskirts of Swanage.

Cross straight over the road and ride down the lane ahead past Swanage Farm, bearing left past Godlingston Manor to head south to cross the railway line – a born-again railway run by enthusiasts complete with steam trains – and come up to the main road by Herston Cross.

6. Turn left here for half a mile or so, until you come to Combe. Just before the turn-off to Langton Matravers, a track goes left past a stonemason's yard. Follow this bridleway on a gentle uphill with fields on both sides, bearing left and then right round the isolated South Barn to head due west on the Priest's Way, an old track which provides excellent riding through quiet country, though slow down for the sheep!

The lonely chapel which guards St Alban's Head provides sanctuary at all times.

7. The Priest's Way track continues all the way to Eastington Farm, where the bridleway bears right across a grassy field which is usually packed with sheep. Ride on to the road at Compact Farm, where you turn left downhill towards Worth Matravers, passing the tiny Square & Compass pub which is worth a visit. The tiny village itself has a small shop and pretty green which you may care to look around, before riding on past West Farm and on to Renscombe Farm, where the road comes to an end.

8. Here there's a sign and noticeboard directing you to follow the track to the left which leads to St Alban's Head. This is a two mile ride on a good hard chalk surface, passing a quarry and eventually coming to the small Norman chapel in a windswept position, with a line of coastguard cottages the only habitation nearby. In foul weather this is a wild place to be, but you can always shelter in the peaceful chapel; in fair weather the views down the coast are the business and point the way this ride will continue westwards.

9. Having taken in the view, ride back along the track to Renscombe Farm where they normally offer fresh milk and other farm produce for sale. Go straight ahead through the gate down the tarmac track ahead, steeply downhill and bearing round to the left to join a muddy track at Hill Bottom. Here you can turn left and ride down to Chapman's Pool, a small, enclosed bay beneath the cliffs. It's marked as bridleway on the OS map, but on my last visit the gate was locked due to danger of cliff falls.

10. The circuit continues in the other direction along Hill Bottom, heading north-west along the bottom of this narrow valley. Much of the riding is tricky here, with rock and mud littering the narrow tree-lined trail, and then a short, steep uphill at Coombe Bottom by the side of Swanworth Quarries brings you up to a track. This leads out to the road by Afflington Barn.

11. Turn left here, and ride along the road a mile or so to Kingston, passing the Scott Arms pub and carrying straight on ahead with the church on your left. Ride on for about another mile – the road goes nowhere, but the bridleway turn-off is not signposted. Look out for a gateway on your left set in some trees, which is marked as a Toll on the OS map though there's no one to take your money. Turn through here, and then follow the bridleway to the right up the side of a field, going through a gate and following the top of the hill along the side of Polar Wood with fine views over Encombe House set in the valley below.

12. The track follows the ridge round to a trig point at the top of Swyre Head – this is a magnificent position much visited by walkers, and with tremendous views over the Dorset coastline it makes a great place for a picnic.

From Swyre Head go through the gate to join the track that continues to the north-west, with a boundary wall on one side and more great views over Kimmeridge Bay with its lonely tower on the headland.

13. The bridleway soon goes steeply down the side of a field to join the road, and from here it's worth turning left to ride down to Kimmeridge Bay, which is a very pleasant spot in summer or winter, much favoured by divers and windsurfers. It is also almost totally uncommercialized, being on privately owned land.

Ride back up the road from the bay, following it right and left up the hill by Kimmeridge Farm, and then taking the left fork for Steeple. A few yards on an unmarked bridleway goes off to the left, going due west along the top of a field towards the Army's Danger Area on the border of its firing ranges at Tyneham.

14. When you reach the red flag and padlocked gate with the Army noticeboard, it's the end of the road. An inviting track lies ahead, but if you try to ride on it you'll probably become cannon fodder or get locked up as a spy. According to the OS map the bridleway turns north-west here, but in practice it's neither signposted or obvious. Head diagonally downhill across the grass field, and at the far bottom corner you'll find the bri-

dleway track which leads bumpily downhill to Steeple Leze Farm and out onto the road.

15. From here you've got four miles or so on-road, though with gentle ups and downs and hopefully not much traffic it's relatively pleasant. Turn right towards Corfe, and when you've passed through Church Knowle look out for the bridleway track that goes up to the left. This comes just after a 90 degree left hand bend, and leads you up to the foot of Knowle Hill where it turns right and follows a track all the way along the bottom of the hill into Corfe.

16. When you hit the road just outside Corfe, bear left downhill with the ruined castle towering above you. A track goes round the base of the castle to the right; it's a footpath so you have to walk, but it's a better alternative than riding round by the main road.

This path brings you to the centre of Corfe, which is an interesting place though very touristy. If you've time do check out the castle (National Trust), which is a fine ruin in an almost impregnable position, which was eventually slighted by Cromwell's men during the Civil War.

Places To Visit:
Corfe Castle ruins NT
(tel: 01929 481294);
Swanage Railway
(tel: 01929 425800);
Chapman's Pool;
Kimmeridge Bay.

Top Pubs:
The Square & Compass at Worth Matravers;
The Scott Arms at Kingston;
The Fox Inn at Corfe Castle.

Studland Heath

Mainly Offroad

Area: Studland Heath and Nine Barrow Down, to the west of Studland at the eastern end of the Purbecks.

OS Map: Outdoor Leisure 15 – Purbeck; Landranger 195 – Bournemouth, Purbeck and surrounding area.

Route:
Shell Bay (GR:035863)
Greenland (GR:017843)
Studland (GR:037825)
Ballard Down (GR:033812)
Nine Barrow Down (GR:001813)
Rempstone (GR:989829)
Purbeck Forest (GR:994850)
Greenland (GR:017843)
Shell Bay (GR:035863)

Nearest BR Station:
Branksome/Wareham.

Approx Length: 12 miles (19km).

Time: Allow 3 hours.

Rating: Moderate. It's a good climb up the two downs; expect mud in the Purbeck Forest if it's wet; some of the tracks on Studland Heath have a bike-unfriendly surface of sand and soil.

This a companion ride to the Isle of Purbeck Circuit (Ride 1), visiting Nine Barrow Down together with a tour of the flatlands of Studland Heath and the Purbeck Forest, with little time spent on-road. Beware that during summer the chain ferry that connects Shell Bay to the Sandbanks peninsula can develop serious car queues (going to Studland in the mornings and back in the late afternoon), so don't approach the area by car!

1. Start at the Shell Bay car park on the south side of Poole Harbour entrance, a couple of hundred yards from where the Sandbanks chain ferry lands. Follow the long, straight road ahead through fine countryside (at its best when car-less); there is a bridleway running parallel, but in practice it's a sand and soil track which is very bike unfriendly.

2. After a couple of miles where the road bears left, look out for a signposted bridleway turning off to the right. Turn down here and follow the hard, fast track to the bridleway T-junction at Greenland where there are a couple of houses. Turn left through the narrow NT gate which has the word 'Bridleway' written on it. Head straight on through several similar gates and past a barn, turning left where bridleway blue daubs indicate the options of left and straight ahead. Here you head diagonally across the field, through a couple more NT bridleway gates.

3. Head on across Studland Heath National Nature Reserve in a south-east direction. There is a fair amount of boggy ground, and as you cross over towards Studland village it becomes increasingly sandy which is bad news for your brakes and gears. On your right you'll see the unusual looking Agglestone Rock – said to have been dropped by the devil when he tripped over Old Harry – and then you head down into trees, bearing right across a stream which has a narrow bridge over it. You may meet horses here.

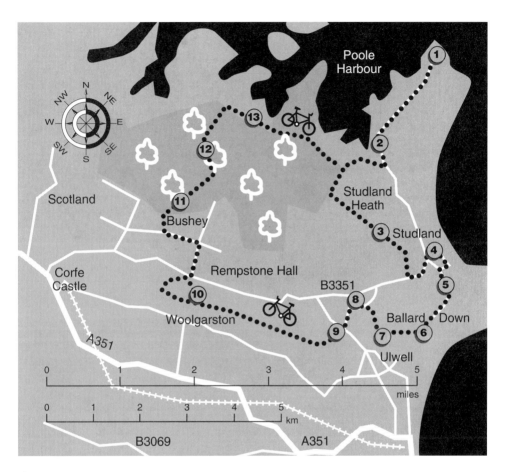

4. The track leads up round the back of the Knoll House Hotel, past some buildings, and then comes to a crossing track with a gate complete with blue daubs on the left. Turn up the gravel bridleway track to the right, and almost immediately left again. The section which follows could be the muddiest of the ride and is usually badly chewed up by horses from the nearby stables, but is short.

5. This track leads out onto Agglestone Road where you turn left until you hit the main road, turning left and then forking right to pass the Manor House Hotel and Bankes Arms pub. From the pub head down the hill,

round the bend to the right, and up to the farmyard. Here, turn left up a rough road which heads straight up the hill to the Glebe Estate as you follow the same route as Ride 1.

6. Carry straight on up past the houses of the Glebe on your right, until you come to the last one which is a large, red brick, two-storey affair. Here bear right and then left up through a gate and onto a track past the NT sign. Go on up the hill, and eventually you'll come to a stone seat marked 'Rest And Be Thankful' with a fine view over Poole Harbour and Bournemouth Bay as far as the Isle of Wight, and also over to Swanage.

25

7. Turn right through the gate here, and ride along Ballard Down in a westerly direction. After about three-quarters of a mile you'll come to an large obelisk commemorating the local water board; bear off to the right past it, and head downhill to the Swanage road.

8. Turn left along the road for about one-fifth of a mile. After you pass a road forking up to the right, the road bends left and on the opposite side there's a gate with an NT sign for Godlingston Hill which you can see wending its way up the hillside. Plug up this track which is a long, hard haul; however the going is good as it's on solid ground.

Down. If you overshoot there's another connecting bridleway going down the hill through gorse further on. Both are steep downhills, eventually leading to the Corfe–Studland road.

10. At the road go straight over and on down a minor road past Rempstone Farm, following the road left and ignoring narrow roads ahead and to the right. This crosses the route of Ride 3. You pass Rempstone Old Farm on the bend, and then some way on come to houses on the right and left where you turn right down an unmarked track. If you overshoot you will come to a telephone box and a few more houses – it's about one mile on-road.

Despite the rugged nature of Studland Heath, there are good tracks with old stone signposts.

9. At the top, bear left by the old gun emplacements, following the sign and keeping west along the top of Nine Barrow Down. The going is mainly on grass, and you soon pass over Ailwood Down marked by NT signs, and then on along Branscombe Hill with Corfe Castle ahead.

Look out here for a bridleway track going down the hillside to the right. It's about 25 yards before a gate by an NT sign for Ailwood

11. Head down this track, and when you come to a smallholding on the left there is a bridleway sign showing you the way to go to the right through a gate and across a field.

Turn right at the next sign, and then ride along what was once a narrow gauge railway line and is now a very pretty track lined with old pine trees and blazing gorse in the spring. Some of the going is muddy but it's mostly easy; just keep straight on in an ENE direction

The farmhouse at Newton, which is passed along the way on this route.

and you'll come to a tarmacadam crossroads.

12. Head straight over here, and onto a rough road with a sign saying 'BP Vehicles 20mph Only'. Keep on along this forestry road, and you'll come to a bridleway crossroads indicated by daubs of blue paint. Turn left through thicker trees, and when you break into the open follow the bridleway sign straight ahead, through a gate, and across a field.

Cross to the far side, then turn right along its perimeter, keeping to the left down a track which can become very muddy. Ower Farm is to your left, and you may also see a couple of the 'nodding donkeys' which work the older oil wells in this region.

13. Keep on along this track which winds round Newton Bay, a very pretty spot which would be fine for a stop. Ahead you'll see a large old farmhouse which is Newton, marked on the OS map; head for the right-hand corner of the building where the bridleway gate is,

and then out onto a track where you bear left, keeping left and following the bridleway signs past Goathorn Farm. Here ignore the bridleway blue daub pointing straight on across a muddy field, and bear right with the track past Greenland, taking the left turn at the bridleway junction to rejoin the outward route and get back on the Shell Bay road.

Places To Visit:
Corfe Castle NT
(tel: 01929 481294);
Brownsea Island NT
(tel: 01202 707744).

Top Pubs:
Bankes Arms or Manor House Hotel in Studland;
cafe at Shell Bay.

Arne Penisular and Corfe

Mainly On-Road

Area: The east end of the Purbeck Hills.

OS Map: Outdoor Leisure 15 – Purbeck; Landranger 195 – Bournemouth, Purbeck and surrounding area.

Route:
Corfe Castle (GR:959822)
Ulwell (GR:022807)
Studland (GR:036823)
Rempstone (GR:987822)
Wytch Heath (GR:970845)
Arne (GR:973882)
New Mills Heath (GR:960840)
Corfe Castle (GR:959822)

Nearest BR Station: Wareham.

Approx Length: 20 miles (32km).

Time: Allow 3 hours.

Rating: Easy. Virtually the whole length of the route is on quiet roads. A few hills, but nothing too serious.

This is an agreeable ride, and particularly suitable when persistent rain has made offroad trails unusable. At the height of the summer you may find a lot of cars wiffling around and generally getting in your way here, but on a sunny weekday out of season you'll probably find the roads much more to your liking.

1. You can start this ride from Corfe, or alternatively from Studland. Both have car parks, but tend to fill up with car-borne trippers during the summer holidays. If you start out early, you should avoid them.

From the Square in the centre of Corfe close to the entrance to the Castle (NT), ride down the hill bearing left on the Wareham road. After a short distance take the first right turn near the bottom of the hill, bearing right on a narrow lane that leads uphill under the disused railway arch.

2. This lane leads you out past Challow Farm, along a narrow (mostly one car wide), little-used road that follows the bottom of the down all the way to Swanage. Alternatively if you want to go up and offroad, it connects to the bridleway leading along the top of the down; this later drops down to re-join the road by Godlingston Hill, a short way to the north-west of Ulwell.

If you stick to the road it's pleasant riding. Few cars come this way, and there are gentle ups and downs and twists and turns which keep things interesting. If you change your mind and want to go up, there are also bridleways leading to the top of the down at Woolgarston and Knitson. Don't confuse the bridleway which runs along the side of the hill with the one on top – the former can be muddy and hard going.

3. At Knitson the road heads away from the down, directly towards Swanage. Unless you feel a great desire to visit that busy seaside town, take the next left turn past Godlingston Manor, passing the solitary cemetary and then turning left again by the improbably sited

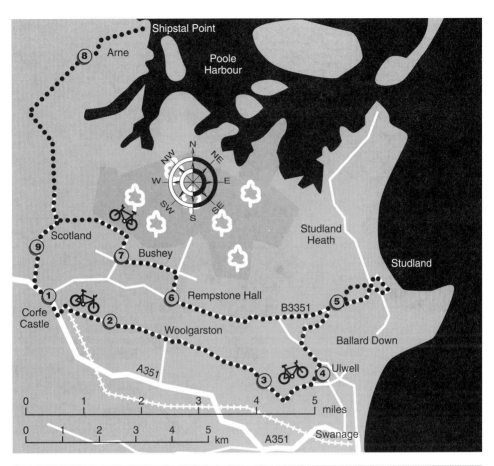

The view over Swanage from 'Rest And Be Thankful' at the top of Ballard Down.

Corfe Castle (above and opposite) dominates the landscape for miles around, but the village itself suffers from cars.

Redland brick works – a well hidden piece of industry in the middle of nowhere. This brings you down past the Ulwell caravan and camp site, where there is a cafe/pub/restaurant with a good reputation, and onto the main Swanage–Studland road.

4. Turn left here, following the road to the start of a steady uphill. The next left turning leads up to the Corfe road; you can ride up this way if you want to cut out some distance and not visit Studland.

Otherwise, follow the road on uphill. A bri-

dleway off to the right leads up to the top of Ballard Down by a mini Cleopatra's Needle which is a water company monument, while the road itself goes up and then downhill into Studland, where you can turn right for a tour of the village which can supply drinks at either of its three shops, or at the Bankes Arms pub or Manor House hotel. If you like churches, the Norman one here is pleasantly tucked away and worth a visit.

5. From the Studland crossroads, follow the Agglestone road straight ahead to rejoin the

Corfe road by Woodhouse. From there you've got about three miles on the Corfe road – this is pleasant up and down riding with fine views out over Poole Harbour, only marred if there are a lot of cars about.

Past the golf club and just past Rempstone Hall (set back on the right side of the road behind a long, long beech hedge, and apparently boasting a 22,000-acre back garden!), look out for the first turning on the right at the top of a rise.

6. Turn off here, bearing left past Rempstone Farm and following the quiet lane through the tiny hamlet of Bushey. Take the next right turn at a T-junction, joining a bridleway (tarmac road) which bears left along the side of woodland. Cross straight over at the next road, joining the bridleway track that bears right through the woodland by the side of Wytch Heath on a good surface. Watch out for the special road built for the oil tankers here, and then follow the bridleway on across an open field which can be heavy going with a mixture of sand and mud to clog your back wheel.

At the next gate the bridleway follows the side of a grassy field, dipping past a brook, and then bearing left on a track to join the road at South Middlebere.

7. Turn right here, and follow the road past Hartland Moor and Slepe Moor all the way to Arne. If there are not too many cars it's lovely riding through moorland and woodland in an area which is largely unspoilt. Arne itself is a tiny place famous for its bird sanctuary and nature trails; its name is derived from the Saxon word 'Aerne' meaning a secret place. Other attractions are the delightful church of St Nicholas (which is always open) where the blue frontal represents the seas of the world, and the somewhat incongruous toy museum and next door cafe.

8. From Arne itself a bridleway leads down to the shoreline at Shipstal Point. This is pleasant riding, but take it easy as it's 'the walk' for all the car-borne trippers here, and it also enters the bird sanctuary. The beach at Shipstal Point could be delightful for a picnic.

9. From Arne there are a number of routes back to the main Wareham–Corfe road. For Corfe it's predictably best to follow the signs for Corfe, with Corfe Castle coming into view as you ride past New Mills Heath.

This brings you out onto the main road by the new roundabout a short distance from Corfe centre; it's easy enough riding back to the start point, but it seems a shame that the old disused railway can't be a cycleway, rather than the 'maybe some time in the future born-again railway' that it's marked out for.

Places To Visit:
Corfe Castle ruins NT
(tel: 01929 481294).

Top Pubs:
The Fox Inn at Corfe Castle;
The Bankes Arms or Manor House
Hotel at Studland.

Corfe and Kimmeridge

This makes an excellent companion to the Arne Peninsula and Corfe ride, heading west rather than east and suffering rather less traffic. It can be a 100 per cent on-road ride – and as such is excellent – though there are some bridleway options which could extend the ride both in time and distance. We'll come to them later!

1. From the centre of Corfe ride round the north side of the Castle, following the road signposted to Church Knowle, and checking out the gunnery range signpost to make sure the roads are open. Ride on through Church Knowle which has a pleasant enough pub, and then take the next left signposted to Kimmeridge.

2. This is a lovely, narrow lane, which past Bradle Farm heads steadily up the south side of the Corfe River valley with fine views opening out behind. At the top there's a T-junction, with Kimmeridge Bay way downhill to the left.

3. Follow the road on a steep downhill, bearing right and left through Kimmeridge village which has a small cafe that boasts it's open all year round. Beyond the houses you come to the toll for the private road that leads down to Kimmeridge Bay – the toll is for cars and bicycles go free (thank you Smedmore Estate) – which is a fine place famous for its rocky reefs and Clayel Tower on the headland. It's popular with surfers and windsurfers if the waves or wind are right, and also popular with more enterprising motorised tourists who sit in their cars while gazing at the view.

4. What goes down must go up, and it's a fairly steep slog back to the top of the hill where a bridleway goes westwards towards Tyneham, but doesn't quite get there due to the Army firing ranges. Follow the road on downhill past Blackmanston Farm, turning left for Steeple and then plugging up in a very low gear to the top of West Creech Hill. Here you often hear the crump, crump, crump of the Army's guns, and it's wise to check that this part of the ride isn't

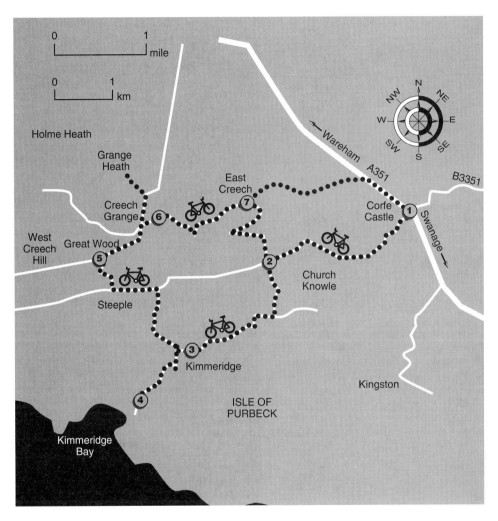

closed before you set out. If you're lucky the road that continues westwards towards Povington Hill and down into Tyneham may also be open. Tyneham is a wonderful place; a forgotten village which was occupied by the Army during the war and never returned to its owners. Sad for them, but for us it means the ruined village and its surroundings are preserved in a timewarp that is recorded in fascinating detail in the beautifully preserved church. All credit to the Army for not commercializing Tyneham – you can't even buy an ice cream there, which is just the way things should be.

5. From West Creech Hill follow the road west along the top of the down above West Wood with wonderful views over Poole Harbour, and then oh so steeply down towards Creech. This is a great downhill, but remember to grab your brakes at the bottom as it's worth stopping for a look at the entrance to Creech Grange which looks like a truly desirable Jacobean mansion.

Looking west over Kimmeridge. In this part of Dorset the Purbecks give wonderful views over the coastline.

6. From here there are options. You can turn for home, following the road due west from Creech Grange to East Creech, and then ride back over Stonehill Down to re-join the Corfe road on the outskirts of Church Knowle.

However at this point I decided to investigate some nearby bridleways, though I have to admit they were not totally satisfactory. The first led north-west off the road a short way beyond Creech Grange, heading towards Grange Heath and Holme Heath. At first it started well, joining a hard track past the cricket pavilion by the Breach Plantation and looking set for a good ride ahead. The problems come when you hit the heath, which becomes more and more boggy and wet as the bridleway deteriorates into a maze of little tracks. I strayed way off course, drifting to the north and getting onto another bridleway up by Doreys Farm, a track that proved seriously muddy and was well ripped by tractor tyres.

Whether the Grange Heath/Holme Heath bridleway picks up again I have no idea. On the map it continues through to East Holme, with a large gap in the middle where there is a track shown but no bridleway. The Army owns the land all around here which may make finding your way across tricky, but if you're game for adventure it could be worth a go.

7. There is another bridleway option. A short way to the north-east of East Creech, the map

shows a bridleway going due east through Norden Wood to join the Wareham–Corfe road on the outskirts of Corfe. It's easy to find your way along here and it passes through delightful woodland, but when I rode it the track was extremely muddy and more importantly appallingly cut up by mountain bike tyres.

I met an elderly walker who commented on the damage bikes had done in an aggrieved but fairly friendly way, and it was impossible not to agree with him. The lesson seems to be to avoid this track – horses don't appear to use it, presumably because it comes out on a fairly busy road – or at least push your bike and take it very easy in wet/muddy conditions, giving way and being as polite as possible to all walkers.

At the end it comes out into the open by a caravan/camping site. Ride carefully through here (watch for children) to join the road, where you'll find you can follow an old forgotten road for a short way towards Corfe – it's the way roads should be!

Places To Visit:
Corfe Castle ruins NT
(tel: 01929 481294).

Top Pubs:
The Fox Inn at Corfe Castle;
The New Inn at Church Knowle.

Chaldon Down and Lulworth

This is a classic tour of West Purbeck, starting out along the Dorset coastline, swinging inland for some woodland riding, and returning to the start point after a fine ridge ride. There's plenty of interest along the way, but being exposed to the weather it's best left for fine, sunny days when you can make the most of the views.

1. The National Trust car park above Ringstead Bay is a good place to start from. It's reached via a narrow road turning westwards (signposted to Ringstead) off the A353 a mile or so south of Poxwell to the west of Weymouth, and is a good base for exploring Ringstead Village and Bay – by foot, as there are only footpaths down to them. As an alternative you could start the ride from Lulworth; there's a free car park at Lulworth Camp near the southeast corner of the route.

2. From the Ringstead Bay car park, follow the hard white chalk track eastwards along the top, through the gate, and downhill past South Down Farm which we're told is being run by the National Trust in an environmentally friendly manner. Past the next gate keep left; it's easy to stray off onto the clearer track which runs due south to Holworth House above Burning Cliff, but this is not a bridleway as the locked gate testifies.

3. The bridleway runs along the top edge of the field on the south side of Chaldon Down, heading downhill on the grassland of The Warren with fine views of Lulworth Cove opening out ahead. Past a strange pair of beacons, the bridleway joins a hard track, eventually heading on a fast downhill to join the road at Daggers Gate.

4. There's a good track which goes straight on from here to Lulworth Camp via West Dean Farm; alternatively if you want to visit West Lulworth with its picturesque pub and cafe, turn right for a pleasant enough pedal on-road, finding your way to Lulworth Camp with a steep climb up the B3070 – don't take a photo

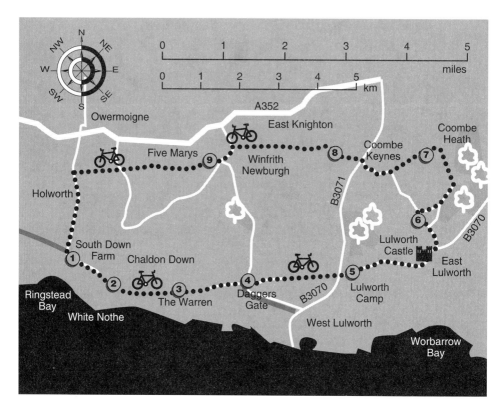

of the tank at the top, or the Army will throw you and your bike in the lock-up!

5. Lulworth Camp is all Army tank land, and the pleasant road that goes east to East Lulworth has a free car park about halfway which gives a view of the proceedings; this could be an alternative place to start the ride from, but once again don't take photos! Riding into East Lulworth you pass the huge park of Lulworth Castle on the left, bearing left through the chocolate box village and left again to join the quiet road for Coombe Keynes.

6. Less than a mile along here you pass a crenellated lodge just before the road heads downhill towards a phone box. Opposite this turn right up a track (signposted as a bridleway) and follow it into the woods to the north of

Home Farm. After an odd kind of dog-leg the track follows the south-east side of the ornamental lake, before turning north by the side of Coombe Heath. Here you wind through a small patch of old woodland, before hitting a strange area of wild, open land by the side of a forest. The tracks are confusing – and potentially very wet – but if you keep right you'll soon hit the main track, bearing left towards an isolated house in the far trees (very boggy here!), before hitting a hard track in the woodland.

7. Riding through the woodland, take the first track on the left and follow it out of the woods and on across an open field towards Coombe Keynes. Once again navigation is not totally obvious, and you need the OS map and a good sense of direction to find your way to the track that joins with the road.

National Trust information boards describe the views over Ringstead.

Follow the road through Coombe Keynes here, turning right onto the main road and then left after about 100 yards to join a hard track that goes downhill toward woodland. Follow the bridleway signs left into Coombe Wood (it's a popular place for the local deer), breaking out across fields with the Atomic Energy Establishment at Winfrith dominating the skyline to the north.

8. Keeping east, this will lead you to the road at Winfrith Newburgh. Turn left here and ride through the village as far as the church; then take a right opposite the church green, joining a farm track which heads up the hillside. A short way up, bear left as indicated by the bridleway sign; it's shown as a footpath on the OS map, but I was lucky enough to bump into the local Rights-of-Way Officer at this very point, and he confirmed it was a bridleway.

9. This takes you on a fine, grassy ridge ride, heading west past Five Marys and Lord's

Barrow. Cross straight over at the first two road junctions, and then at the third (due south of Owermoigne) turn left onto the road and follow it downhill south as far as the farmstead in the dip at Holworth. It's a dead-end road so you're unlikely to meet much traffic; just past the duck pond at Holworth it runs into a bridleway track, with a short, steep uphill on concrete leading to the top of the down with fine riding ahead for the remaining mile or so back to the start.

Places To Visit:
Lulworth Castle EH
(tel: 01929 41352).

Top Pubs:
The Red Lion at Winfrith Newburgh;
The Castle Inn at West Lulworth.

The Hardy Monument

Mainly Offroad

Area: Far west end of the Purbecks, between Weymouth and Dorchester.

OS Map: Landranger 194 – Dorchester, Weymouth and surrounding area.

Route:
Ringstead Bay (GR:760823)
White Horse Hill (GR:715845)
Hardy Monument (GR:616878)
Portesham (GR:602858)
Abbotsbury (GR:577853)
Nottington (GR:656823)
Preston (GR:696828)
Ringstead Bay (GR:760823)

Nearest BR Station: Broadwey (Weymouth).

Approx Length: 32 miles (51km).

Time: Allow about 5 hours.

Rating: Moderate. The riding is mainly straightforward, but it's a good distance and you need to keep an eye on the map.

This is a fine tour of the Dorset countryside between Dorchester and Weymouth with big views most of the way. I chose to start from the Ringstead Bay car park to link it to the Chaldon Down and Lulworth route, Ride 5; this adds a dog-leg of some four miles each way, which can be cut off if you start from anywhere else on the circuit – Abbotsbury or even central Weymouth would make excellent alternatives.

1. From the Ringstead Bay car park head west down the hill (potentially fast, but narrow and well used by cars) to the main A353 just south of Poxwell.

Turn right, and then where the road bends left look out for the bridleway sign on the left which is directly opposite a track (footpath) on the right. The bridleway here leads steeply uphill (a pushathon) across grassland, crossing straight over the track leading to Poxwell Manor by a dilapidated barn. Past here the bridleway bears left, and is more up than down as you head for the top of White Horse Hill where the trig point measures 158m.

2. Once on White Horse Hill, join the hard track ahead, passing the grave of 'Gentle Ben – A Faithful Friend', and joining the road that runs WNW past Came Wood.

This is fairly car-free and pleasant enough riding. When you come opposite the golf course, look for the bridleway that forks left, leading you on a bumpy, winding track downhill and under the railway, and then on to the main A354.

3. Turn right here. Thankfully it's not too far – just a short way uphill and then take the first track on the left which is bridleway and part of the long-distance Dorset Coast path. Follow the track on past the A3159, and along Corton Down with the great tower of the Hardy Monument coming into sight on top of the hills ahead. It's good riding here and easy to find the way; but expect to pass a few horses, and show due consideration.

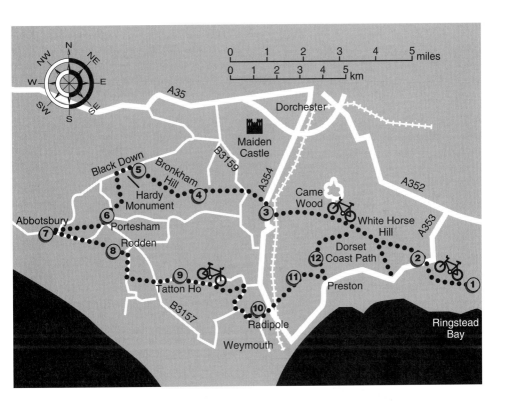

4. Past Bronkham Hill a switchback of ups and downs soon leads down to the Martinstown road at the foot of the Hardy Monument. Turn left for a short, sharp uphill to the base of the Monument which looks like a lighthouse stranded in the middle of the land. It's enormous, and was built to commemorate Admiral Hardy of 'Kiss me, Hardy' fame, not the equally famous writer, Thomas Hardy, who lived up the road in Dorchester. Take care here – the loose gravel of the Monument car park had me off my bike in front of an assembly of parked motorists.

5. This is a good place to picnic or ruminate; when you're ready to move on, ride along the road westwards past the Monument, turning down the first track on the left (unsignposted bridleway) by the side of trees. This dives southwards down through delicious woodland, to emerge in a clearing at the bottom by dis-

used, ruinous farm buildings. Go straight ahead steeply up the other side, bearing right through a gate to join the bridleway that leads over the top of Portesham Hill and down into the village of Portesham, with fine views over the coastline ahead.

6. Ride on through Portesham, taking the B3157 signposted to Abbotsbury, and then turning onto the first track on the right side of the road by some buildings. This isn't signposted as bridleway, but if you bear left and right it leads you onto the old railway which runs straight along the hillside into Abbotsbury. It hasn't been touched up at all and remains in surprisingly good condition, with a few emotive reminders of what the railway must have been like in its day, chugging through the quiet countryside.

7. Abbotsbury is a popular place with car-borne tourists – equally famous for its Gardens and Swannery, and romantically dominated by St Catherine's Chapel on the hill. It has a choice of pubs and cafes plus a few shops, and with a large, free car park on the east side would make a good alternative start point for this route.

Once you've exhausted Abbotsbury, which could eat a few hours, take the B3157 eastwards out of the village, and turn right onto a track; this is just beyond a couple of buildings, and is once again unsignposted bridleway. Follow it to a gate where there is a bridleway sign, and follow its direction up the side of Linton Hill ahead, bearing due east to follow the side of the fields along the hillside with the occasional narrow gate showing the way; this section can be well churned up by horses and cattle in wet weather and could be grim going.

8. Crossing a grassy field, the bridleway joins a track leading into the hamlet of Elworth. Bear right to head further south here, joining a bridleway that brings you over the hill and down into Rodden. Bear right on the road to head due south some more, riding through open countryside and hitting the top of the hill where you turn left onto the bridleway that runs along Rodden Ridge (unsignposted again).

This will take you eastwards with great views over the Chesil Beach, bringing you to the B3157 by a waterworks. Ride straight on along the road ahead for about two miles, passing Tatton House and Farm and taking the dead end road on the right for Buckland Ripers.

9. Follow this downhill and across the stream, leaving the road for a track which goes past a beautiful small chapel and then going offroad across fields. The way is not too obvious here, and I got no help from a lady on a horse who made a good job of ignoring me! The track will lead you to the road on the outskirts of Nottington. Turn right, but take care as it's blind in both directions. Ride south towards the outskirts of Weymouth, and be prepared to deal

The Hardy Monument can be seen from far off along the Dorset Coast Path.

with cars as you bear east towards Radipole.

10. When you've crossed the River Wey, take the first turn on the left before you hit the main A354. Ride up the side of Corfe Hill, and at the top bear right into the first dead-end terraced lane which leads to the big main roundabout ahead, where bikes can get through but cars can't. This is a severely busy roundabout with a superstore on one corner, and is something of a nightmare to cross. You want to get to the north-east side, where a bridleway is clearly signposted going north-east beneath the railway towards Littlemoor.

11. At first the track here runs straight and true, and the horrors of Weymouth's car population are soon left behind; sadly the surface is pretty grim to ride on, alternating between potential severe mud and 'improved sections' covered in rubble. The track comes to an end as it breaks out of the trees at the foot of a hill, and there is no clear indication where to go.

Just keep on up the right side of the fields, reaching the top of the hill with a belt of trees on the right. You'll find a gate which leads down to an unsightly new housing development on the outskirts of Littlemoor; keep on the right side of this, and then follow the road straight down to Preston which doesn't take long.

12. You could get back to Ringstead Bay car park on the main road, but with a long, long uphill and heavy traffic it's not recommended. Instead, about 100 yards before you reach the main A353 take a left turn, leaving the neat houses behind to head up by the side of Chalbury and Green Hill, with a bridleway track (Dorset Coast Path) connecting with the outward route at the top of White Horse Hill.

Poor pooch – a lonely monument to a favourite dog on the top of White Horse Hill. The 'horse' is cut in chalk on the south side.

Places To Visit:
Abbotsbury Tithe Barn
(tel: 01305 871817);
Abbotsbury Swannery
(tel: 01305 871684);
Abbotsbury Sub-Tropical Gardens
(tel: 01305 871387).

Top Pubs:
The Ilchester Arms at Abbotsbury (plus cafes);
The Smugglers at Osmington.

Abbotsbury to Litton Cheney

Mainly Offroad

Area: The west Dorset coast, to the north of Abbotsbury.

OS Map: Landranger 194 – Dorchester, Weymouth and surrounding area.

Route:
Abbotsbury (GR:578853)
Littlebredy (GR:590890)
Litton Cheney (GR:553907)
Abbotsbury Castle (GR:557863)
Abbotsbury (GR:578853)

Nearest BR Station: Dorchester.

Approx Length: 13 miles (21km).

Time: Allow 2–3 hours.

Rating: Moderate. It's a good climb out of Abbotsbury, and a steady climb out of Litton Cheney.

This is a short but excellent ride taking you over some magnificent countryside to the west of Weymouth. Be prepared for hills, and if it's clear look out for the magnificent views. Much of the distance is offroad – in dry weather the going is OK, but after wet weather some sections could be pretty dismal. Abbotsbury has a very handy car park on the east side of the village and is a good place to start this ride; alternatively you could base it on Litton Cheney where there is a YHA hostel.

1. From the car park in Abbotsbury, cross straight over the main B3157 taking a short uphill to join the upper road where you turn right to head north-east. This is the start of a long and fairly steep climb up the side of White Hill by Abbotsbury Plains, with the views getting bigger and better as you near the top. There is an optional bridleway which cuts the corner on the way up – it's not at all clearly marked, and with such a severe uphill you're better staying on-road.

2. Where the road levels out, follow it round to the right ignoring the bridleway signs which fork off to the left. A short way on take the first road turning on the left; this is bridleway, and you soon bear right onto a hard track which leads north along the top of Crow Hill towards an isolated farmstead.

3. This farmstead was in the process of being 'done up' when I last rode by, and is in a magnificent position. The bridleway leads round the left side of the buildings, and then continues due north across open high ground, following an indistinct trail. Keep with it as it starts to head downhill, going fairly steeply down the hillside with the splendid mansion of Bridehead coming into view below. Join the track which leads past the left side of the cricket ground to the road on the outskirts of Littlebredy.

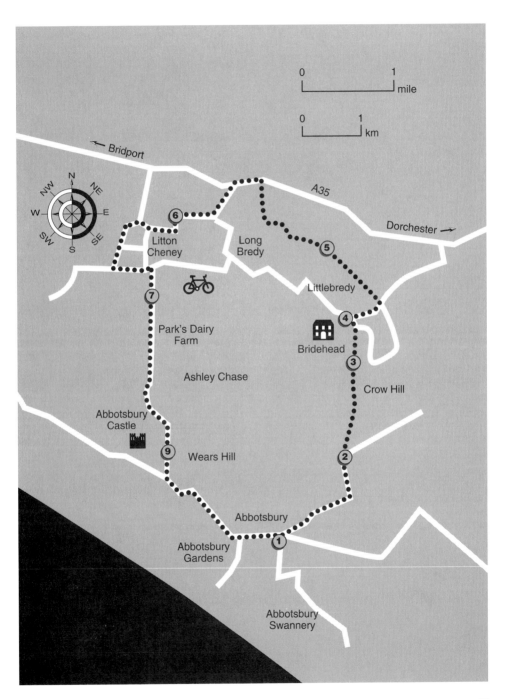

You'll find this interesting relic on the hard climb up the hill on the outskirts of Abbotsbury.

4. Littlebredy is very picturesque and well worth a ride around. Once you've taken it in, follow the road uphill past the phone box, heading east-north-east up to the top of White Hill where there are two clearly signposted bridleway tracks heading off into the distance on the left side of the road.

5. Take the left of these bridleway tracks, and follow it along the top of Whatcombe Down in a north-westerly direction. If the weather is good it's fine riding up here, as you pass various tumuli and inquisitive cattle, keeping on in much the same direction to the Long Barrow on Martin's Down. Here the track seems to disappear in an area which could be very muddy in wet weather. The correct route bears right

round the side of the big tumuli, joining the A35 on a concrete track which heads down the short hillside.

6. Thankfully you've only a very short distance on the A35, before taking the first left turn which plunges down towards Litton Cheney at very high speeds. When you get there, Litton Cheney is a real picture postcard of a place with its pleasant pub sited next door to the strange old YHA hostel (tel: 01308 482340) which is in a cheese factory.

7. From the youth hostel follow the road south and then due east, taking the second left turn signposted to Park's Dairy Farm. Keep due south past the farm, joining a track which plugs steadily up to the top of the hill where it meets the tarmac road leading down into Ashley Chase. Keep on riding south, with a final uphill leading to the hill fort of Abbotsbury Castle – close by is a replica of the beacon which was lit to signal the arrival of the Spanish Armada.

8. From Abbotsbury Castle it's a short ride down to the B3167, where a great downhill leads virtually all the way to Abbotsbury. Hair-raising speeds may be obtained, but watch out for cars and be sure you arrive safely in Abbotsbury where in the summer season a wide choice of refreshments await you.

Places To Visit:
Abbotsbury Tithe Barn
(tel: 01305 871817);
Abbotsbury Swannery
(tel: 01305 871684);
Abbotsbury Sub-Tropical Gardens
(tel: 01305 871387).

Top Pubs:
The Ilchester Arms at Abbotsbury;
The White Horse at Litton Cheney.

Litton Cheney and Bridport

This is a useful ride linking Litton Cheney with Bridport. Both could be start points, and both have YHA Hostels which are handy when planning a series of car-unassisted rides moving east or west across this part of Dorset. The road-riding here is generally very pleasant; the offroad trails can be muddy, difficult to find and consequently frustrating, but when they're good they're very good and the bad memories are all left behind.

1. From the pub and youth hostel at Litton Cheney, take the road that heads due west past Four Meads Farm. This is very pleasant riding on level ground with few cars about, but the bridleways hereabouts are not so pleasant – the two that turn north opposite Berwick and Modbury Farms (where you can buy the farms' own cream) soon become seriously muddy and/or difficult to follow, even if the weather has been dry.

2. So keep on and take the next right past Bredy Farm, a very splendid looking place which has its own museum. Follow the road north on a slight uphill, and then turn left (due west) on a quiet lane that leads steadily downhill into Burton Bradstock. There's a bridleway about a third of the way along this stretch – once again it's dismal riding, and the same is true of the next bridleway that leads due north from Burton Bradstock.

3. From Burton Bradstock follow the road north towards Shipton Gorge. After a long, steady uphill this road swoops down and then up again. At the next crest take the left turn signposted to Bennett's Hill Farm, which is the start of a magnificent offroad section leading west along the hilltop towards Bothenhampton and Bridport with tremendous views opening out ahead. It eventually plunges down the hillside to join the road on the southern outskirts of Bridport – take it easy here as it is a popular area with dog walkers.

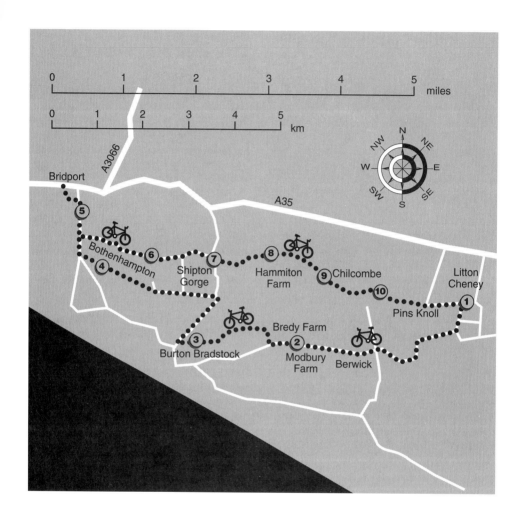

4. Turn right along the side of the road, and at the next roundabout you may care to ride into Bridport which is a pleasant enough town with a YHA hostel (tel: 01308 22655) in a former flax warehouse by the side of the River Brit. Alternately bear right at the roundabout, and then take the next right off the main road into Bothenhampton.

5. Old Bothenhampton is a kind of forgotten village on the outskirts of Bridport, and very pleasant it looks too. You'll pass one fine

church on the way up the hill, and further on it's well worth forking left to view the second church which is now disused but is a lovely little building in a fine setting, and very peaceful.

6. Follow the lane on due east past the last of the houses, and you'll come to the local refuse tip. Not the most beautiful place to go cycling, but a bridleway leads round the left side and continues on up the next field to join a hard track which leads on to Shipton Gorge. Be warned that the first section of bridleway here

could be very muddy, signposting is non-existent, and you may lose the way.

7. Once you hit Shipton Gorge opposite the
recreation ground, the pub is a short way uphill
to the left. To continue the ride head straight
on past the church and then take the road that
continues due east past Lynch Farm. This is the
start of a difficult offroad section, and at this
point you may prefer to head south on-road to
rejoin the outward route from Litton Cheney.

8. Past Lynch Farm the road drops downhill
and then bears uphill to the left. Just past a
turning to Hammiton Farm, look out for a well
overgrown bridleway gate on the right. The bridleway follows the side of woods to cross a
stream (wet here), continuing to follow the
north side of the woods across a couple of fields
before joining a track to the east of Hammiton
Farm – this is a frustrating section as this track
leads directly from the road, but the way is
barred by 'Private' signs when you reach
Hammiton Farm itself.

9. The bridleway heads south past a large
pond, and then bears east up the side of a field
towards Chilcombe. With no track this is very
heavy going and a definite pushathon, though if
you're in no hurry the surroundings are pleasant
enough. At the next gate a track leads up to a
solitary, modern farmhouse near the top of the
hill close by a cattle grid, with the exclusive set-
tlement of Chilcombe a short way uphill.

10. The signposting is non-existent, but the
bridleway continues straight on eastwards,
going downhill across the next field, crossing a
stream at the bottom where you'll more than
likely encounter extreme mud, and then climbing up to join a good track beneath Lower
Coombe. This speeds you on to the road at
Pins Knoll, from where it's an excellent downhill all the way into Litton Cheney at the end of
an interesting ride.

The small church on the outskirts of Bothenhampton
is no longer in use, but is a delightful reminder of former times.

Places To Visit:
Bridport Museum and The Chantry
(tel: 01308 422116);
The Old Farming Collection at Bredy
Farm (tel: 01308 897229).

Top Pubs:
The Three Horseshoes at Burton
Bradstock;
The White Horse at Litton Cheney.

Charmouth and Marshwood Vale

On-Road and Offroad

Area: South-west Dorset, along the coast from Charmouth and inland.

OS Map: Landranger 193 – Taunton and Lyme Regis.

Route:
Charmouth (GR:365933)
Wootton Cross (GR:379960)
Higher Park Farm near
Marshwood (GR:392989)
Paddock's Cross (GR:426977)
North Chideock (GR:420939)
Morcombelake (GR:401940)
Charmouth (GR:365933)

Nearest BR Station: Axminster.

Approx length: 15 miles (24km).

Time: Allow around 3 hours.

Rating: Moderate. Parts can be very muddy in wet weather; some good hills.

Charmouth is a small, hillside town on the main A35, boasting a Heritage Coast Centre and Guided Fossil Hunting Walks along the cliffs; it is also the start and finish point for this pleasant ride around the Marshwood Vale area in the extreme west of coastal Dorset. The main Charmouth car park is likely to act as an overflow for the beach-side car park in the main summer season, but has loos and all-day parking at a modest price.

1. Turn east downhill through Charmouth, and then take the first left turning signposted to Wootton Fitzpaine, crossing the A35 by-pass. The road heads uphill past the smart entrance to the church at Catherston Leweston with its Manor House, passing a farmhouse where the road levels at the top of the hill. Just as you start to go downhill take the first track on the right.

2. This is a bridleway heading uphill, and is the start of an excellent offroad section leading up past a dilapidated building and on through a patch of fine trees. It then follows the tree line out across the open grasslands of Conegar Hill with great views to the north. There's no track as such, but the way is easy to follow, heading downhill to cross a track coming up from the valley and following the side of a field up to an old copse of trees on the hilltop. Go through the gate here and there's a pretty downhill section by the side of the woods on a good track, before a more lumpy downhill leads you to the road at Baker's Cross.

3. Go straight ahead for about half a mile to Abbott's Wootton Farms. The bridleway turning here isn't signposted, and there are a number of tracks to choose from. Ride past the farm buildings, and take the track to the right just before the bungalow on the corner. That's the right one, passing by a new and rather fancy farmhouse on the right. The track leads downhill across a field in fine surroundings, and then up towards trees on the hillside ahead where it goes through a gate onto a track running by the

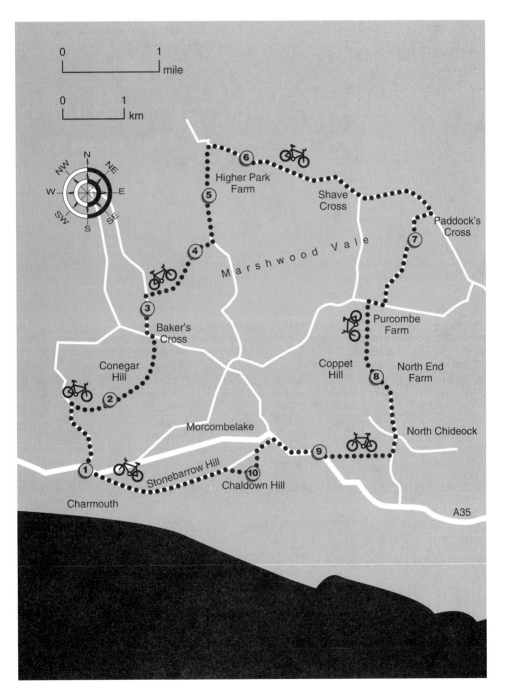

The hilltops above Charmouth afford fine views and a fine ride, but it's a stiff climb up there.

side of the woods. There were some fearsome 'road repairs' with old broken bricks when I rode here, but otherwise it was OK.

4. The bridleway then goes into the woodland of Prime Coppices, following a winding trail – it's all very pretty and would no doubt be delightful to ride in a dry summer, but when it's wet there's a lot of pushing, even when it starts to go downhill! On the far side of the woods a track leads steeply down to some old ramshackle buildings, where a bridleway sign points in an unlikely direction across a stream. Ignore this – it points the wrong way.

5. Follow the lane to the right, past more shanty buildings. Take the next left which leads up to a farmstead. The bridleway goes straight ahead through the cow pen via a couple of gates – there is no signpost, but this is the way to go.

From there on the bridleway carries on due north, keeping mainly to the right side of grassy fields with a wooded valley over to the left. Keep on under the overhead power cables – it's

a slight uphill most of the way, but the going is good until you come to the last field where the bridleway hits the road between Baber's and Higher Park Farm. The OS map shows the bridleway going straight across this field, to come to a soggy old metal gate in the hedge which is marked by a bridleway sign. Riding in early spring, I got the impression that the route had been oversewn; if you find the way barred by crops, you have every right to press on .

6. Turn east along the road for some quiet countryside pedalling, which is mainly downhill and fast going to the pub at Shave Cross, a decent looking place to stop at about the halfway stage of the ride. Past the pub ride on eastwards, and after about a mile opposite Paddock's Cross take the next lane on the right which has a mountain bike-friendly dead-end sign. The windy lane heads downhill between high hedges to Stoke Mill Farm, where you pass a cute little wishing well with resident gnome by the roadside, before joining a track that starts as cinders and soon deteriorates to serious mud if it's been wet. This brings you under the power-lines once again, eventually leading on a slight uphill to Purcombe Farm on a section which when I rode it had some monumental mud.

7. Turn right through the farmyard – it's still bridleway. Just past the next farm buildings turn left onto a track going up the hill. All I could find to show the way here was a footpath sign lying on its side; further up the hill there are bridleway signs showing that you are indeed on the right and legal trail. It's a good track leading up the side of Coppet Hill, and then running south across grass just below the summit with its trig point at 157m. The route continues as pleasant riding for some distance, but then just as you're downhilling towards North End Farm a bridleway sign sends you down to the right on an extremely bike-unfriendly detour. This follows a sunken, overgrown path between the fields – it was a total bog when I rode it, and likely to be pretty miserable whatever the conditions.

8. Not before time it leads out by the side of North End Farm. Ride straight ahead along the lane here, which is more of the 'best of England' quiet countryside riding that this area is so good for. At the next junction a bridleway turns off right up Hardown Hill; I opted to miss this one, having had enough mud and preferring to do my hillclimbing on-road. Ride on south-wards to the next right turning, by some fine old farm buildings near Chideock Manor. From here it's something over half a mile of steady pedalling up to the main A35; thankfully you can't really see it or hear it as you grind up-wards. When you get to the top it's another matter though. This road can be seriously busy, and getting across requires patience and care.

9. Safely on the other side you pass the Moores Dorset Knob factory. For anyone who doesn't know, these crumbly delights are well worth investigating and are particularly de-licious with cheese, so hop off your bike and see how they make them because it's open to visi-tors on weekdays.

From here it's thankfully only half a mile's pedal along the A35, which is fast riding on a steady downhill with the best part of the entire route left to last. Just past the pub on the op-posite side of the A35, fork left onto a dead-end lane that soon heads uphill. Ignore the left track signposted to Golden Cap, but when you come to the next houses look out for the bridleway signposted steeply uphill to the left. This tells you it's the way for horses and bikes to go to Charmouth, even though it's not shown on the OS map.

10. The uphill is a bit grim – steep, narrow and likely to be well churned by horses. However, once you're up on top of Chaldown Hill it's worth it – fine riding on grass and hard tracks, with fantastic views over the coastline. The National Trust notice board further on tells you all about the Golden Cap Estate, and claims that the views from here extend from Start Point off Plymouth to Dartmoor inland.

Follow the bridleway route along the top of the down, joining a hard track – be prepared for cars coming up to the car park here – and then bombing along the top of Stonebarrow Hill and steeply down towards Charmouth, a descent that unfortunately can't be record breaking as it's too steep, too narrow, and there may be cars coming up the other way. Back in Charmouth, which is a nice little place, there are all sorts of cafes, tea houses and pubs, or why not ride on down to the beach (there's a cafe here too) and cool off with a post-ride swim?

> *Places To Visit:*
> Charmouth Heritage Coast Centre
> (tel: 01297 60772);
> Moores Dorset Biscuits
> (tel: 01297 489253).
>
> *Top Pubs:*
> The Shavecross Inn at Shave Cross;
> other pubs and cafes at Charmouth.

Dorset Inland

Dorset Inland is a place of quiet countryside and farmland, connected by small and often charming villages. On the east side it's mainly flat while to the west it's distinctly hilly, but wherever you ride there's a get-away-from-it-all feel to this area where even the 'capital' town of Dorchester is as relaxed and pleasant as any big town can be. There is a huge selection of country roads and bridleways to choose from. Some of the tracks are excellent while others are unforgivingly mud-strewn in wet weather, but that's all part of the fun of exploring this quaint corner of England. So ride out on your bike and have fun on the thirteen routes that follow.

Ride 10: The Great West Dorset Cycle Ride

Ride 11: Thomas Hardy to Lawrence of Arabia

Ride 12: Maiden Castle and Hardy's Monument

Ride 13: Beaminster Westwards

Ride 14: Beaminster Eastwards

Ride 15: Maiden Newton and Sydling St Nicholas

Ride 16: White Giant Ride

Ride 17: Buckland Newton to Piddletrenthide

Ride 18: Blandford Forest

Ride 19: Wareham Forest

Ride 20: Winterborne Tour

Ride 21: Badbury Rings Ride

Ride 22: Cranborne Chase

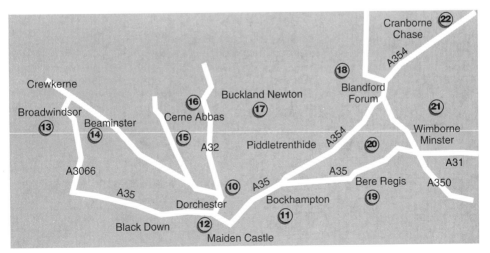

The Great West Dorset Cycle Ride

Mainly On-Road

Area: Inland, north and west of Dorchester.

OS Map: Landranger 194 – Dorchester, Weymouth and surrounding area.

Route:
Dorchester (GR:690900)
Puddletown (GR:755943)
Glanvilles Wootton (GR:676082)
Yetminster (GR:598109)
Evershot (GR:575045)
West Milton (GR:501962)
Shipton Gorge (GR:500915)
Litton Cheney (GR:549900)
Hardy Monument (GR:612877)
Martinstown (GR:641890)
Dorchester (GR:690900)

Nearest BR Stations: Dorchester, Yetminster.

Approx Length: 65 miles (105km).

Time: Allow 6–7 hours plus stops.

Rating: Moderate. It's a good length, and the south-west corner of the route has plenty of hilly country. As a road route it is extremely successful in avoiding heavy traffic for much of the distance.

The Great West Dorset Cycle Ride has been created by West Dorset District Council as an ideal cycle route for touring the area. It works well, providing a long but very pleasant day out on mainly quiet roads. For the enthusiast there are offroad options; though even if you're fit, it has enough small hills to be a demanding circuit without leaving the road. The route map published by WDDC is recommended for this ride, and is cheap.

1. Dorset's capital town of Dorchester is an obvious place to start the ride; it could as easily be started from Yetminster at the northern end of the circuit, Bridport on the south-west corner, or any of the many villages in between.

The official route guide recommends that you start at the Tourist Information Centre in the middle of Dorchester, and then follow the Wareham signs out of town en route to Bockhampton. This is OK if you don't mind putting up with initial traffic on the A352. If you prefer to start more quietly offroad, there is a bridleway that runs eastwards out of Dorchester between the River Frome and the railway line – to find it turn left off the first roundabout signposted to Wareham, and follow St George's Street under the flyover. It's not ideal, as it runs along a narrow, potentially muddy track by the side of the municipal tip, but it misses out the A352 and gets you to a quiet road which is back on the route to the west of West Stafford. A short way on turn left for Lower Bockhampton.

2. The official route goes due north on-road, but there's a very pleasant bridleway option which turns left along the river at the second bridge, passes Stinsford where Thomas Hardy's heart is buried, and continues to Higher Bockhampton where the great man was born and where you can visit his cottage.

3. The route follows the south side of Puddletown Heath, turning north to cut the

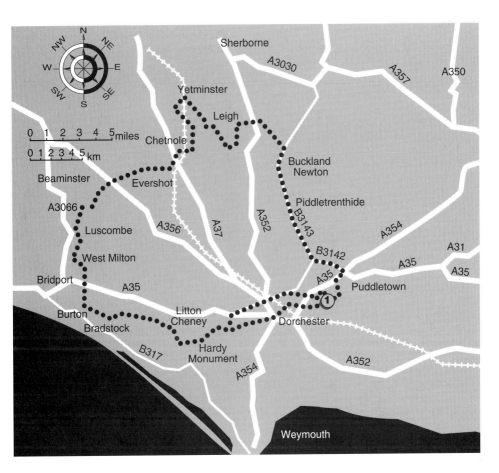

corner of Puddletown Forest along a road known as 'Rhododenderon Mile'. This is a steady uphill which must be at its best when the rhododenderons come out in May; if you prefer to opt for a more interesting offroad alternative, try the bridleway track that runs due north through Ilsington Wood. Both road and track lead to Puddletown.

4. Puddletown is surprisingly interesting and pleasant (*see* Ride 11). From here the route follows the valley of the River Piddle northwards along the B3146 to Glanvilles Wooton. This is a quiet road with the most gentle of ups and downs, often coming close to the river as it

passes through countryside that is pleasant rather than spectacular, and visiting the Piddle-related Piddlehinton and Piddletrenthide along the way.

5. At Buckland Newton the route temporarily leaves the B3143, turning left to head past the church (the pub is a short way south here), a very fine rectory, and other imposing Victorian buildings, with some up and down riding adding some views and some zest to the route.

From here the ride continues through the Vale of Blackmoor, following the B3146 west to cross the A352, where it joins what was once a private road leading to the village of Hermitage

55

Evershot is a fine village and it makes a welcoming place to stop.

– its name derives from the Hermitage of Blackmoor religious group who lived here 600 years ago. If you fancy more offroad, look out for the alternative bridleway from Higher Holnest to Hermitage.

6. The route continues on to Leigh where there's a pub, and then to Yetminster at the northern end of the route – a fine-looking small Dorset town on a hillside, served by British Rail with a couple of pubs and a handful of shops.

From Yetminster the route follows a minor road southwards across flat country, running parallel to the railway which it crosses at Winterhays, passing on through Chetnole and by the side of the Wriggle River. A short way on from Hell Corner – you can't imagine how it lives up to that name – the next right turn at Redford leads south-west to cross the A37, with hills looming ahead and about to transform the ride.

7. Next stop is Evershot, where the first thing you'll find is a convenient stone-carved seat under a big tree by the entrance to Melbury Park – it's an excellent place to stop and look at the map, and work out what comes next. Evershot itself is the finest village on the ride, very handsome, and well worth a look at; you'll find the pub in the high street up the hill, with the church a short way beyond.

8. Beyond Evershot the route continues west to cross the A356 – for cyclists a fast, dangerous road – followed by a steady climb on the B3163 up Toller Down. What goes up must come down, and a fast downhill leads from the top of Hackthorn Hill with Beaminster just over a mile distant. However the route turns south here and never quite gets to Beaminster, so be ready to hit the brakes ready for the left turn at the bottom of the hill. This is signposted to Mapperton Manor and Gardens, and is where the official route guide warns that there are hills ahead and offers an alternative 'easy route' through the

Brit valley to the west of this up and down area.

9. Mapperton's gardens are open to the public during the summer months (afternoons only), and will no doubt attract the two-wheeled naturalist. From there the route wriggles and writhes southwards through a sort of 'little Switzerland' landscape, exploring a series of super-narrow roads which offer great riding for enthusiastic cyclists so long as you can be sure there's not a car coming the other way.

10. Don't miss the sharp left turn down Jack's Hill – at this point amazing views start opening out ahead right over the English Channel. The surroundings from here on are very attractive with plenty of picture postcard views along the way, visiting the out-of-the-way hamlets of Loscombe and West Milton, before coming to Loders and Uploders which both have the advantage of pubs.

11. A steady climb leads uphill to cross under the A35. The route then heads southwards and downhill past Shipton Gorge, and on through a fine open landscape to Bredy Farm with its display of old farm implements by the side of the road – the bridge across the River Bride here is in a perfect setting, and the farmhouse rates as quite 'exquisite'.

12. The route now turns east alongside the River Bride, heading through flat country to Litton Cheney where the YHA hostel (tel: 01308 482340) is sited in an old cheese and milk factory, conveniently next to the very pleasant pub. From here it continues east through Long Bredy, heading back into the hills up past Kingston Russell House, en route for Littlebredy – with its own private gate by the roadside, this hamlet must have a claim to being one of the most picturesque places in Britain!

13. Ride on past the Littlebredy church, forking right out of the hamlet to climb steadily up the side of the valley, with the 'big house' at Bridehead coming into sight below. Past

Littlebredy Farm there's the steepest climb of the whole 65-mile ride, before the route heads along the top of the Black Down ridge, following the signs to the Hardy Monument.

14. There are fine views all round from the Hardy Monument, but the penalty is that you can expect a good deal more motorized traffic to be around on this last part of the ride. The official route guide tells you that it's all downhill from here; that's not quite true, but it does start with a long downhill towards Martinstown. From there on the going is fairly flat as you ride to Dorchester – if you prefer to finish offroad, an optional bridleway track leads due east from Clandon Barrow to the north of Maiden Castle with its wonderful, concentric, defensive rings.

The Great West Dorset Cycle Ride route map is available from Tourist Information Centres in West Dorset. It's printed on water-resistant laminated paper, and has a map and clear route guide with comments on places visited. Contact *West Dorset TIC, 1 Acland Road, Dorchester. Tel: 01305 267992.*

Places To Visit:
Dorset County Museum (tel: 01305 262735);
Hardy's Cottage at Higher Bockhampton (tel: 01305 262366);
Ilsington House (tel: 01305 848454);
Athelhampton House and Gardens (tel: 01305 848363);
Mapperton House and Gardens near Beaminster (tel: 01308 862654);
The Old Farming Collection at Bredy Farm between Burton Bradstock and Litton Cheney (tel: 01308 897229).

Top Pubs:
The Thimble at Piddlehinton;
The European Inn at Piddletrenthide;
The Acorn Hotel at Evershot;
The White Horse Hotel at Litton Cheney.

Thomas Hardy to Lawrence of Arabia

On-Road and Offroad

Area: East of Dorchester.

OS Map: Landranger 194 – Dorchester, Weymouth and surrounding area.

Route:
Higher Bockhampton (GR:725922)
Puddletown (GR:755945)
Briantspuddle (GR:816930)
Clouds Hill (GR:824909)
Affpuddle Heath (GR:805923)
Admiston Farm (GR:767933)
Tincleton (GR:766920)
Higher Bockhampton (GR:725922)

Nearest BR Station: Dorchester.

Approx Length: 21 miles (34km).

Time: Allow 4 hours.

Rating:
Fairly easy. Not much in the way of hills, and the offroad tracks are mostly good, even in wet weather. Navigation is fairly straightforward.

This is a particularly good ride if you are of a literary or historical disposition, since it connects the homes of two great men – the cottage at Higher Bockhampton on the outskirts of Dorchester where the novelist and writer Thomas Hardy was born, and the cottage at Clouds Hill where 'Lawrence of Arabia' lived out his final days in slightly eccentric seclusion. Both these houses are administered by the National Trust and open to the public; even if you've no interest in them, it's an enjoyable ride in its own right.

1. Hardy's birthplace at Higher Bockhampton has a small car park nearby for those who arrive with their bikes strapped to a motor. Alternatively it's an easy ride from Dorchester where there's a BR station – find your way to the south-east side of the town, and turn off the main Wareham road (A352) onto a minor road heading due east for West Stafford. Turn north to cross the River Frome to Lower Bockhampton (Hardy lived out his later days at Max Gate near here – the house is also administered by the NT and open to the public). From there you will find a handy bridleway that runs from Kingston Maurward and Stinsford, with their two fine mansions, to Higher Bockhampton. The distance is about three miles from the centre of Dorchester.

2. Hardy's birthplace is a small cottage, situated up a track well off the road on the west side of Puddletown Forest. When it's open you can view the garden but theoretically you have to make an appointment to see inside where Hardy's early great novels were written. You may turn up and find the house open to visitors without prior appointment, but be wise and don't bank on it.

3. Hardy's garden is a pleasant place to sit and consult the map, ready for the offroad section through Puddletown Forest. This is a popular area for bikers with tracks, trails and plenty of hills, and with plenty of good viewpoints it's

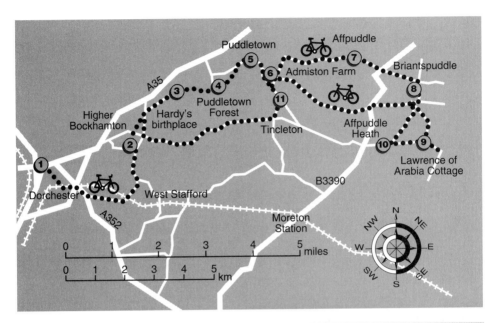

reasonably easy to find your way without getting lost. From Hardy's birthplace, follow the track that goes due east past the Hardy Monument erected by American admirers.

A gentle uphill on a reasonable surface takes you to a maze of crossroads and no sign-posting; with one eye on the map and a good sense of direction you should find your way through the forest, keeping in more or less the same direction to join a hard forestry track which zooms down the side of Green Hill to join a very minor road by The Kennels.

4. Turn left then almost immediately right here, joining a track (which is bridleway) that leads to The Kennels. You'll pick up the bridle-way crossing track after a short distance; turn left here across a faintly unappetising rubbish tip, to join a narrow track that winds its way through woodland by the side of The Kennels itself, a rather splendid house in high Victorian style that was being 'done up' from a ruin when I rode by. At the far side of the woods follow the bridleway straight on across a bumpy field, joining a farm track. Here you join the road (the

A monument erected by Hardy admirers from America stands near his cottage.

59

Thomas Hardy's birthplace is a picture-postcard cottage today, though perhaps it was not so idyllic in his lifetime.

gate seemed well tied up despite it being a bridleway); ignore the track which carries on in the same direction, but effectively leads to nowhere.

5. Follow the road downhill to the main road (A35) at Puddletown. This is the sort of place that appears doomed by the traffic that speeds through its centre, but it's worth taking the time to explore the north side of the village which is relatively well protected from the A35, and has some fine architecture, including the over-immaculate houses that surround Ilsington House, a very smart pile which is sometimes open to the public.

6. From Ilsington House follow the A35 for no more than a few yards eastwards, before taking the first right turn signposted to Tincleton. (Alternatively, just before you make this turn you'll see a track going due south. This is a pleasant bridleway that leads through Ilsington Wood, and even though it's a very indirect way of following the route you may like to explore it.) After less than a mile on the road, turn left into the driveway of Admiston Farm, with its fine looking house set back from the road. The

drive is not signposted as a bridleway, but the bridleway leads past the farm, bearing right and leading up to a small thatched cottage on the edge of the woods. Turn left here through a gate, following the bridleway up the side of a field and into very pretty woodland, to join a track that drops back down to the A35 close to Athelhampton House (privately owned, and also open to the public).

7. There's no need to hit the A35 here. Just before you reach it, turn right onto a track that runs by the side of the slightly dilapidated church. This track leads eastwards following the course of the River Piddle, passing Park Farm and Southover House before coming to Affpuddle. Here you join the B390 for a short distance uphill, bearing off to the left by a thatched corner cottage to follow the road to Briantspuddle. You'll know you've hit Briantspuddle when you pass a 1930s style executive housing estate with a memorial, twin rows of immaculate thatched houses and lots of burglar alarms. Ride on into Briantspuddle proper, where you take the first right signposted to Bovington.

8. This road leads uphill through woodland, passing two appetising looking bridleways. Cross straight over at the next road junction, riding along the dead straight road past Throop Heath. Take the next right turn (signposted to Bovington), and almost immediately on the left there's a poorly signposted bridleway that cuts the corner of Tonerspuddle Heath on the way to Clouds Hill. This is a weird place to go riding, since it also doubles as a tank training ground; it's also quite hard riding whatever the weather conditions, which may make the road the preferable option.

9. The bridleway leads out onto the road opposite Clouds Hill, the strange little house where Lawrence worked in comparative obscurity. If it's closed you can't see much since it's well hidden by trees and bushes, but if you continue on down the road you'll come to the spot where Lawrence was killed, trying to avoid two boys on bicycles when blasting by on his motorbike.

10. From Clouds Hill turn left onto the road for Dorchester. After just under a mile, look out for a track that runs north-east through the woods and across Bryants Puddle Heath, passing Rimsmoor Pond and coming out onto the road by Cullpeppers Dish south of Briantspuddle. Turn left here, and follow the road along the top of the down heading west across Affpuddle Heath. Cross the next road, joining a wide track that goes straight ahead between Sares Wood and Marl Pits Wood. This continues westwards past a trig point, crossing Southover Heath on an easily followed track through woodland. The going here is mostly pretty good, with just a few potential muddy areas if it's been wet.

11. Eventually the track breaks out across an open field (keep right here), dropping downhill to follow the side of woodland back down to Admiston Farm. Retrace your wheel tracks here, but turn left at the end of the drive, following the road (very quiet riding) south to

You can see little of Clouds Hill from the road, so make sure you arrive when it's open!

Tincleton, and then west towards Dorchester, which will lead you back to Higher Bockhampton. On the way you will pass a bridleway track that leads into the south-east corner of Puddletown Forest, by the side of a small cluster of houses – if you prefer to finish the ride offroad and find your own way home, this is the way to go.

Places To Visit:
Hardy's Cottage NT
(tel: 01305 262366);
Ilsington House
(tel: 01305 848454);
Athelhampton House and Gardens
(tel: 01305 848363);
Cloud's Hill NT
(tel: 01985 847777).

Top Pubs:
Try your luck in Puddletown.

Maiden Castle and Hardy's Monument

Offroad and On-Road

Area: South-west of Dorchester.

OS Map: Landranger 194 – Dorchester, Weymouth and surrounding area.

Route:
Dorchester (GR:693904)
Maiden Castle CP (GR:669889)
Dorset Coast Path (GR:646869)
Hardy Monument (GR:616877)
Littlebredy Farm (GR:600883)
Black Down (GR:610877)
Portesham (GR:608858)
Corton Down (GR:635867)
Martinstown (GR:648889)
Maiden Castle CP (GR:669889)
Dorchester (GR:693904)

Nearest BR Station: Dorchester.

Approx Length: 15 miles (24km).

Time: Allow 3 hours.

Rating: Easy/Moderate. A few minor climbs; good tracks; a well signposted ride through fine country with some big views.

This is a great ride. The tracks are really good and should be OK in wet weather. You pass through some fine country and the bridleways are clearly marked or signposted most of the way, with plenty of brilliant views out over the Dorset coastline in good weather.

1. From the centre of Dorchester take the signposted turning for Maiden Castle off the A354 Dorchester–Weymouth road on the town side of the by-pass. Drive or ride until you reach the car park at the foot of the Maiden Castle earthworks. This is a splendid iron age fort composed of massive concentric ditches. There's an information panel in the car park which makes interesting reading, and it's worth a walk round the fortifications to see what their builders achieved, and what attackers were up against.

2. Go through the gate by the car park and ride up the hill to the right hand side of Maiden Castle. When you reach the padlocked main gate and kissing gate entrance to the fortifications with an English Heritage sign, bear right and pick up the bridle track which continues round to the left with a blue blob showing you the way. Follow this track round the north-west side of the fortifications with Hog Hill on your right, and then go through a gate and ride down a valley with Ashton Farm ahead of you.

3. Here you join a minor road for no more than a couple of minutes' on-roading. Bear round to the right, and then keep straight on until you reach a more major road coming from the right a short way on. Bear left here, and almost immediately cross the road and head down to the right on the bridleway track which passes some houses and heads through another farm.

4. The bridleway is well signposted, heading out on a hard chalk track and then bearing left and right into a field – just follow the blue blobs. Keep along the right hand side of the grassy field with the valley on your left, bearing left around the top until you see the bridleway

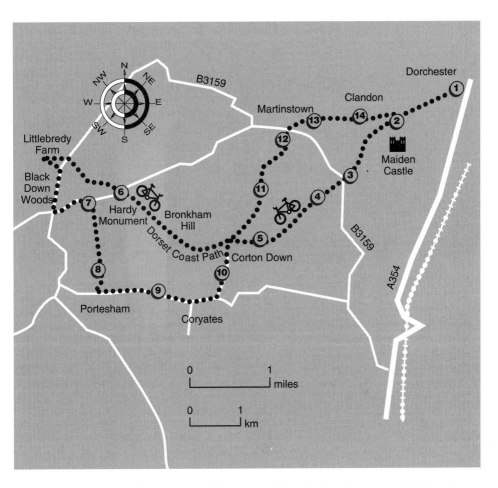

blob on the second gate. This leads to a field which was planted with fully grown corn when I rode through, but a narrow track had been left intact, slicing diagonally in a south-west direction. Head across this field, passing through a grassy section with tumuli to the right, then heading across more of the field until you reach a gate in the corner.

5. Go through and bear left along a clear track which runs along the side of the next field, soon bringing you down to a crossing track bounded by a wall which is the Dorset Coast Path. Ahead there is a fine view south over the Dorset coun-

tryside as it slopes down towards Portland.

Turn right along the Dorset Coast Path, and keep along it bound for the Hardy Monument, a tall, narrow tower which you will soon see ahead in the distance. The Dorset Coast Path is a really good track with fine views on both sides, and there's no way you can get lost! The only vague section is where the track disappears along the edge of a field with Pen Barn Farm – a large, modern farmstead – over to the right. You rejoin the track on the other side of the field, steadily gaining height towards the monument, which makes a fine landmark for navigation.

The Hardy Monument is in a fine, unspoilt position, though be prepared for cars. Unfortunately you can't climb it.

6. Just before you reach the monument, the track goes downhill towards a road. I met an old local on the Dorset Coast Path who had plotted a forty-mile mainly off-road route for the day – he knew the local tracks like the back of his hand, and recommended crossing straight over at the road to try the bridle track that runs through Black Down Woods, and he was dead right. Go straight through the woods, following the bridleway signs on this narrow track. It's a great up and down woodland ride, which after a time breaks into the open as you ride along the head of a valley with the woods still on your left.

Keep on and cross the next road, and then follow the track which bears round to the left before joining a very minor road. Turn left here and you come back to the road you crossed a short time before. Ahead is a track which would take you back towards the monument, but is not shown as a right of way. Instead turn right and then first left to ride east along the road

until the monument once again comes into view.

7. Just west of the monument there is a track going downhill to the right along the edge of a strip of woods. Ride down this, and keep on down into the woods on a really good, fast descent. Carry on downhill and if in doubt bear right, until you come to a clearing in the valley with a bridleway sign over to the left showing another track heading back up to to the monument. Ignore this and go straight ahead through a gate, heading up the steep hill on the other side of the valley and leaving behind a few ruined barns.

8. At the top of the hill the track goes through Portesham Farm, and then bears right downhill and turns to tarmac. Here the ground formations become really unusual with all sorts of hills and hillocks to the right which would make an interesting technical section. You also get a real grandstand view of Chesil Beach, the enormous strip of pebbles running up the coast from Portland.

9. The track soon comes down to a very minor road. Turn left (east) and ramble along, meeting scarcely a car. You pass by Waddon House which is a most imposing building, and a little further on bear left uphill when you join a road coming up from Coryates. Ignore the first bridleway track which goes off to the left at the next right-hand bend. Carry on uphill and join the bridleway a short way on, which goes left alongside the first house you come to with power lines ahead.

10. Keep on up this made-up track past the farmstead on the left, crossing under the power lines once, and then again when the track bends left. Riding over Corton Down you eventually rejoin the Dorset Coast Path on the crossing track that goes on up to Pen Barn Farm.

11. Turn right back along the Dorset Coast Path here, and ride through the next field and

Part of the Dorset Coast Path stretching towards the Hardy Monument in the distance.

through the gate. A little further on there's a three-way bridleway sign. Take the left turn to Martinstown, following the track across a field and then on a long steep descent down Great Hill. The bridleway becomes a proper farm track, and then you reach another 3-way bridleway sign in the valley showing ahead to Martinstown, back the way you came to Great Hill, and an acute left to Bronkham Hill.

12. Carry straight on for Martinstown following the track round to the right. However, don't go up the hill which starts about fifty yards past the sign. The bridleway goes along the left-hand side of the long valley to your right, a turn which is not clearly indicated.

Follow this direction, going through a gate and then gaining height up the side of the valley. At the top turn left through a narrow bridleway gate, and head across the field ahead which brings you back to the farm track. Turn right, and this soon takes you down into Martinstown opposite the church.

13. Here you can go left to inspect the pub. To push on, turn right for a short way along the road, and then turn left at the first turning by a

house called Fishers' Barn. Ride up the hill for about seventy-five yards, and then just past the last house turn right through a bridleway gate. From here ride across a small field, go through a gate, and then along an avenue of trees until you join a minor road.

14. Turn right, cross over the next road which you come to immediately, and go straight offroad onto the track which bears off to the left. Follow this track up to the farm buildings at Clandon – go straight through them and out the other side, passing a small modern house on the left. Maiden Castle and the car park soon come into view. Just keep on downhill, and then turn back to the right for the car park or cycle on into Dorchester.

Places To Visit:
Maiden Castle EH;
Hardy's Monument.

Top Pubs:
Try the pub in Martinstown, or there are pubs, cafes, tea shops etc in Dorchester.

Beaminster Eastwards

**Offroad and
On-Road**

Ride Area: West Dorset, to the east of
Beaminster.

OS Map: Landrangers 193/194 –
Taunton and Lyme Regis/Dorchester,
Weymouth and surrounding area.

Route:
Beaminster (GR:480013)
Langdon Farm (GR:503016)
Beaminster Down (GR:496034)
Catsley Farm (GR:527041)
Benville (GR:543040)
Rampisham (GR:562023)
Kingcombe Crossroads (GR:556008)
Hooke (GR:536001)
Mapperton Manor (GR:505998)
Beaminster (GR:480013)

Nearest BR Station: Crewkerne.

Approx Length: 16 miles (25km).

Time: Allow 3 hours.

Rating: Moderate – there are some
good climbs along the way!

*This makes an excellent companion to the
ride westwards out of Beaminster (Ride
14), and if you're fit you could combine
both in a single day. There are some big
climbs, some big views, a good pub, and
plenty of variety along the way.*

1. From the market place in Beaminster ride
down the hill, and fork left onto the B3163.
Almost immediately take the first left turn opposite the garage by the side of an immmaculate
town house on the corner, and follow this dead-
end road (bridleway) to Langdon Farm. It's
uphill most of the way, and past the farm –
which is a magnificent place with an observatory
in the roof – it gets seriously steep as it climbs to
the top of the down.

2. At the top of White Sheet Hill pause and
take in the view. Turn left as indicated by the
Wessex Way signpost, joining a track which runs
along the top of the down. Turn right when you
reach the road, and then right again at
Beaminster Down, following the quiet road on a
steady downhill and on to join the A356.

3. Ride south-east along the A356 for a short
way, taking the first left turn downhill past
Catsley Farm and on to Benville. From here follow the road to Rampisham, a very smart place
with a Manor House and once-fine inn, which
at the time of writing had closed, turning right
up past the church with a steady grind up
Rampisham Hill towards the radio masts which
dominate the hilltop.

4. Cross straight over the A356 at Kingcombe
Crossroads, following the lane ahead by the side
of the radio masts, and then bearing right to join
the clearly signposted bridleway track which
runs past the south side of the masts. From here
it heads downhill, crossing a field at an angle as
shown by the blue bridleway pointer – look out
for the gate which is well hidden in the overgrown hedge, and follow the bridleway up the
side of the next field to a track which joins the
road above Hooke.

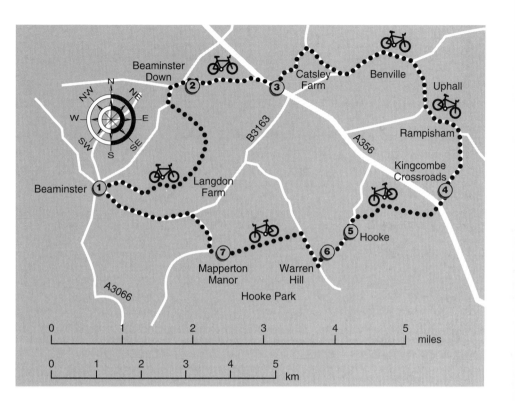

5. Ride down into Hooke (the track that goes straight ahead is not an official bridleway and emerges in the middle of a strange trout farm), and at the church go straight on, following the road south-west up to the T-junction at Warren Hill. Turn right here along the side of Hooke Park woodlands with their strange tree sculpture at the public entrance, and at the end of the woods bear left through a gate onto a track (unmarked bridleway opposite a footpath) that heads up the hillside.

6. This track follows the hillside below Dimstone Hill, keeping to the side of the hedges with magnificent views over Hooke Park to the south. There are no signs but it is bridleway, and at Cotleigh Farm it joins a track which becomes a road, dipping and diving on the hillside above Mapperton Manor.

7. You come out on the road just north of the entrance to Mapperton Manor which is well known for its spectacular gardens. From here it is possible to turn left to seek out the bridleway that crosses the valley westwards towards Beaminster, but if it's late in the day and you're tired the more sensible option is to turn right, joining the B3163 which is fast downhill all the way to Beaminster.

Places To Visit:
Mapperton House and Gardens
(tel: 01308 862645).

Top pubs:
The Greyhound at Beaminster.

Beaminster Westwards

**Offroad and
On-Road**

Ride Area: West Dorset, between
Beaminster and Crewkerne.

OS Map: Landranger 193 – Taunton
and Lyme Regis.

Route:
Beaminster (GR:480013)
Mintern's Hill (GR:035491)
Mosterton (GR:457056)
Clapton (GR:415066)
Burstock (GR:422030)
Broadwindsor (GR:438025)
Stoke Abbott (GR:454007)
Beaminster (GR:480013}

Nearest BR Station: Crewkerne.

Approx Length: 19 miles (31km).

Time: Allow 2–3 hours.

Rating: Moderate. There are some
stiff ups and exhilarating downs, and
a variety of tracks to contend with.

*Beaminster is a very fine small town with
some wonderful buildings, and this is a
very fine ride making the most of bridleways and country roads to the north-west.
The whole area is worth exploring further,
with a network of bike-friendly roads lac-
ing the countryside beyond Beaminster as
far as the Devon border.*

1. Find your way to the market place in the
centre of Beaminster, and turn right off the
A3066 onto a narrow dead-end road which
leads northwards out of the town. Just past the
big new school take the first right fork, and then
follow the right turning signposted to Meerhay
Manor which is a splendid place in a wonderful
setting. The bridleway lane leads uphill past the
Manor through overgrown vegetation, going
fairly steeply up Mintern's Hill to some farm
buildings which were being converted into resi-
dences when I last rode by. Keep on straight
ahead here, joining a rough track which continues as a steep ride to the top of the hill.

2. At the top of Mintern's Hill turn left along
the lane which runs west–east along the top of
the down with fine views out over Beaminster.
Take the next turning on the right signposted to
Chapel Marsh and West Axnoller Farm, passing
a fine avenue of trees on the hilltop and following the signs to Chapel Marsh on a steady
downhill.

3. The lane-cum-track bears left past a barn to
the farmstead at Chapel Marsh. You don't want
to go that far, so on the bend go straight ahead
through a gate, joining the bridleway (unsignposted) which leads along the side of the next
field where it meets a track that leads northwards to the next road. Unfortunately this track
is well 'watered' by the River Axe and can be
desperately wet and muddy, so be prepared for
some heavy going.

4. At the road turn left, riding past Buckham
Mills and the trig point down to Mosterton and
the A3066. Cross the road here and turn right,

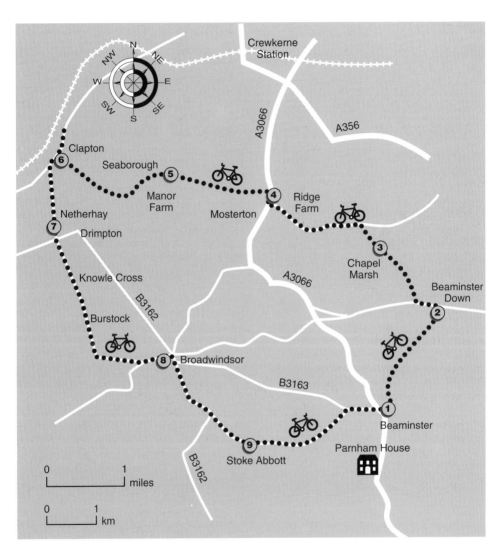

forking left uphill on the next track, and forking left again for West Farm. We had a spot of bother finding the way through the farm here, but the farmer – who was extremely friendly – pointed the way and gave the low-down on the area.

5. Past West Farm the bridleway goes straight across a large field belonging to another farm.

Keep straight on ahead, following the bridleway which joins a track that leads down to the road by Manor Farm on the outskirts of Seaborough, close by the River Axe.

6. Turn left onto the road, and left again by the entrance to Seaborough Court. Look out for the next bridleway on the right which follows the side of the River Axe all the way to Clapton.

Stoke Abbott is a very pleasant place to stop, with a pub that served us good food and beer.

Once past the farm and a number of other buildings, the route heads across fields which could be muddy but are OK when it's dry. The bridleway then joins a track which leads out onto the road on the south side of Clapton. If you're a tradescant offroader, turn right for Clapton Court Gardens which boast ten acres of rare and beautiful plants as well as a cafe.

7. From Clapton head south across the river on the B3165, and just past the old mill bear left onto a minor road which heads due south across mainly flat country through Netherby to Burstock – this is all very pleasant riding.

Past Burstock the road leads up to a T-junction with an overgrown track ahead; turn left here and follow the road into Broadwindsor. (An alternative offroad route could be built-in across Burstock Down.)

8. From Broadwindsor follow the B3162 southwards for Bridport (it's a little confusing finding the way out of town here), taking the left fork onto a minor road at Stoke Knapp, and following it down on a very fast and exciting ride to Stoke Abbott in the valley – this road is very narrow with blind bends, so beware of unsuspecting cars that may be coming up the other way.

9. Stoke Abbott is a charming little place, and the pub is excellent for bikers with a large garden at the back. From here follow the road eastwards to Beaminster – after a fast downhill to the B3163 the road joins the A3066 on the outskirts of Beaminster. If it's the right time of day, you'll find a choice of three tea shops ready to serve you in the market place.

Places To Visit:
Clapton Court Gardens
(tel: 01460 73220);
Parnham House
(tel: 01308 862204).

Top Pubs:
The New Inn at Stoke Abbott;
The Greyhound at Beaminster.

Maiden Newton and Sydling St Nicholas

**Offroad and
On-Road**

Ride Area: West Dorset, to the north-west of Dorchester.

OS Map: Landranger 194 – Dorchester, Weymouth and surrounding area.

Route:
Maiden Newton (GR:598979)
Sydling St Nicholas (GR:632993)
Wardon Hill (GR:612023)
Frome St Quentin (GR:597025)
Cattistock (GR:593996)
Maiden Newton (GR:598979)

Nearest BR Station: Maiden Newton.

Approx Length: 12 miles (19km).

Time: Allow 2–3 hours.

Rating: Easy/Moderate. The tracks are mainly good and easy to follow, but there's a very steep climb out of Sydling St Nicholas.

This is a good circuit in the West Dorset countryside, starting from the small town of Maiden Newton on the A356 to the north-west of Dorchester. It's generally easy riding, but a little care needs to be taken with the navigation.

1. Look out for the fine old school house with its strange clock and the impressive Manor House in the centre of Maiden Newton. The ride starts from the railway station, going under the road bridge to join a track which heads fairly steeply uphill above Combe Bottom. With enthusiasm it's ridable all the way, but before you reach the top look out for a gate on the left where you turn off – if you keep on the main track to the top of the hill, you have overshot.

2. From the gate a track leads straight across a huge field on a slight uphill, coming to a battered collection of farm buildings at New Barn from where it leads out onto the main A37 road. Cross over carefully here, going through the bridleway gate on the other side at the top of Break Heart Hill.

3. The track leads down towards Sydling St Nicholas and is mainly good riding and easy to follow. Near the bottom it turns left and right (the signposting is good), following an overgrown lane which is not such good riding and eventually coming to a potentially very wet and muddy track as it passes Court House on the outskirts of Sydling St Nicholas.

4. Turn left through this village which is sited on the side of Sydling Water. Ride north past the Greyhound pub, and once you've finished with the village keep straight ahead on a dead-end road signposted to Up Sydling. Avoid right turns all the way along here, following the side of the gurgling river to Up Sydling where the bridleway (unsignposted, but opposite a blue post) turns left through the farm and residential buildings. Don't stay with the track which continues due north up Cross Hill.

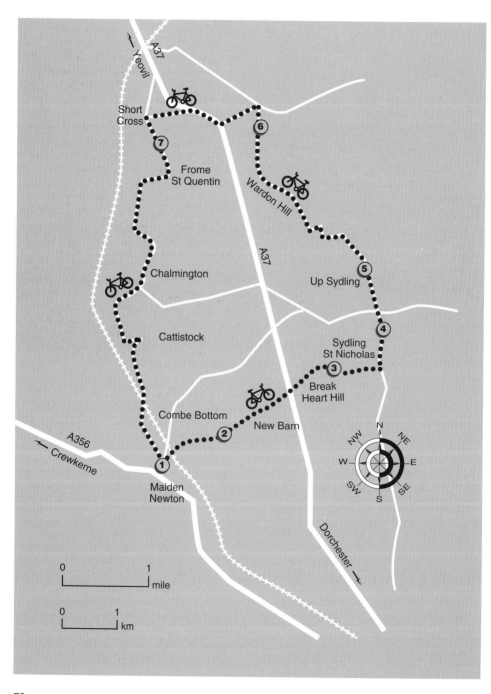

The Greyhound pub on the way out of Sydling St. Nicholas, with the best of the ride still to come.

5. Past the main buildings of Up Sydling take the first track on the right which leads through a heavy metal gate. From there it plods up the side of Wardon Hill, where there are fine views and you'll only have sheep for company. Near the top you come to a rather fine disused barn – from here continue following the track which bears northwards parallel to the A39.

6. The track leads past an old airfield with its disused control tower. This is now used for mini motor racing and clay pigeon shooting, and the noise of high revving engines and shotgun blasts spreads over all the surrounding countryside. You'll hit the road just past the control tower – keep on straight ahead to the T-junction above Batcombe Hill, where a bridleway track leads off westwards to join the A37.

7. Cross the A37, turning right to follow it northwards for a short distance before bearing

off on the first track on the left as the A37 starts to go downhill. This track is a bridleway which leads down to Short Cross, and from here on it's a very pleasant road ride all the way back to Maiden Newton. The narrow road twists and turns and ups and downs its way southwards, passing through the hamlet of Frome St Quentin and coming to the village of Cattistock, where the church is in a classic setting and worth a walk; from there it's a short ride on to Maiden Newton.

> *Places To Visit:*
> Cattistock village.
>
> *Top Pubs:*
> The Greyhound Inn at Sydling St Nicholas.

White Giant Ride

**Offroad and
On-Road**

Ride Area: Mid-Dorset to the north of
Dorchester.

OS Map: Landranger194 – Dorchester,
Weymouth and surrounding area.

Route:
Puddletown (GR:755944)
Ridge Way (GR:720943)
Forston (GR:665955)
Gore Hill (GR:625038)
Up Cerne (657028)
Cerne Abbas (GR:666011)
Piddletrenthide (GR:703999)
Druce Farm (GR:745953)
Puddletown (GR:755944)

Nearest BR station: Dorchester.

Approx length: 24 miles (39km).

Time: Allow around 4 hours.

Rating: Moderate. A few ups and
downs and some of the going could be
seriously muddy in wet weather.

*This is an excellent ride, not least because
it's through very quiet countryside where
you're unlikely to meet more than a handful of walkers or horseriders, let alone any
mountain bikers. Despite the fact that
there is really no hard climbing there are
good views from the top of the ridges, and
there's a choice of pleasant pubs and cafes
in Cerne Abbas where you'll see the
famous 'Giant' on the hillside.*

1. Puddletown, on the A35 north-east of
Dorchester, makes a good start point. On the
west side of Puddletown there are traffic lights
at the junction of the A35 and A354 Blandford
road. About 100 yards west of these lights, look
out for the start of the Ridge Way track on the
north side of the road, signposted by a white
building. This is an ancient road, popular with
local dog walkers, so take it easy. The going is
mainly good as it heads due west away from the
road, though it's steadily and slightly uphill all
the way. Like much of this route, it could also
be very muddy in wet weather.

2. Follow the course of the Ridge Way
straight ahead, crossing the B3143 road. Past a
barn the track goes downhill, and then turns left
and right round the side of a field – the signposting is good, and finding your way is relatively easy.

Keep on across fields towards Charlton
Higher Down. When I rode here the corn had
just been cut and riding over the stubble was
easy, but it looked like there could be problems
at other times of the year.

3. Cross the next road, going straight ahead
down a potholed lane, then following a track
downhill by the side of a large house. At the
bottom the track bears left, becomes overgrown,
and follows the side of more fields from where
another track leads downhill to the road at
Forston by the side of the River Cerne. Turn
right (north) along the road here for a few hundred yards, looking out for the bridleway on the
left just opposite the large farm.

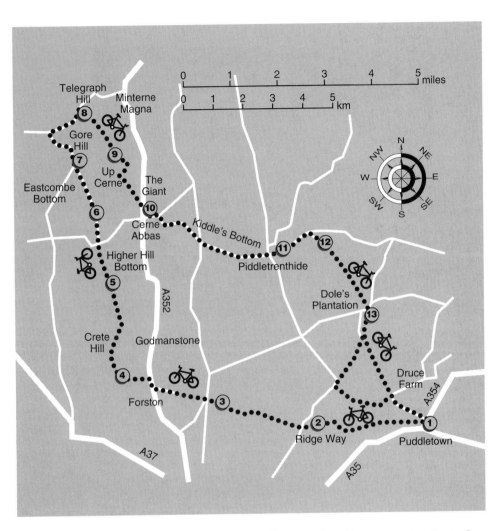

4. Go through the gate here, and steeply up the side of a grassy field where you'll most likely encounter inquisitive horses.

From here a track continues on up a moderately steep grass hill, passing a convenient seat for walkers and then following the top of the ridge. Take the bridleway right turning, signposted along the side of the woods, going through a gate and following a hard track ahead at the start of the long section that takes you northwards to Gore Hill.

5. From here it's just over six miles to Gore Hill, following the top of the ridge all the way with some great views out to the west. It's mainly easy to follow; at the first bridleway crossroads take the right fork towards the trig point on the top of Crete Hill, and then keep on in the same direction past Ridge Hill and Higher Hill Bottom to the next road. The track varies from wide and fast to being fairly narrow, bumpy and lumpy, with parts across plain grass on the top of the hillside.

The ride along the valley to Up Cerne is the prelude to your first view of the giant above Cerne Abbas.

6. At the next road crossing the track continues northwards. It looks better on the OS map than it is, and it's quite slow going. Past Hog Hill the big aerial is a useful landmark, and then the route follows the side of woods between Elston and Wancombe Hill, finally joining a hard, fast surface which swings round the side of Eastcombe Bottom – a big bowl of countryside laid out below to the left – passing a farm, and coming to the road at Cross & Hand not far on.

7. Turn right along the road here until you come to the big car park/recreation area at Gore Hill (GR:637038) which would make a useful alternative place to start/finish the ride – from here the information panel claims you can see as far as the Blackdown Hills (26 miles), the Quantocks (32 miles), the Mendips (34 miles) and Glastonbury Tor (23 miles).

Follow the road to the north-east. Mostly the signposting on this ride is very good; the next bridleway turning is one exception, being completely unmarked and unobvious.

8. About a mile from the Gore Hill car park, look out for a footpath sign on the left. Opposite it on the right, a field slopes downhill towards thick woodland. You can just make out a faint track across the field here, leading to a vague entrance into the woods – go for it! If you reach a sharp right hand bend in the road, you've overshot.

9. Once in the woods, the track heads steeply down, and brings you to another great track in a beautiful valley below East Hill. All too soon it turns to tarmac, bringing you in record time to the immaculate hamlet of Up Cerne. From here follow the road on a quiet, narrow switchback, hitting the A352 where you turn right and almost immediately left for Cerne Abbas.

You can't fail to notice the White Giant on the hillside here. He's 180ft long and thought to be 1,500 years old. He also has a magnificent male member – locals believe he's all about fertility, and that sleeping on the hillside can cure barrenness. Another legend tells that the outline was cut around a giant who was sleeping off the effects of a feast of stolen sheep.

10. Cerne Abbas is an immaculate little place, well tuned in to well-heeled tourists with a selection of cafes and pubs to choose from, and fine buildings including a terrace of near perfect Tudor houses opposite the seventeenth-century church. It is however a fussy place for a muddy biker, and I headed on by turning right uphill for the neigbouring village of Piddletrenthide. This follows a switchback road through pleasant countryside with few cars to worry about, and Piddletrenthide offers the choice of the Piddle or Poacher Inn.

11. For the final section of the ride I followed the road eastwards towards Cheselbourne. After a stiff uphill, the road here levels out with some good views to the north, with the bridleway turning just over a mile from the B3143 turn-off. It's not marked and is not obvious.

12. Opposite a couple of tracks off to the left, look for the driveway to Dole's Ash Farm on the right. Turn onto it, and then follow the bridleway up the right side of the field ahead, passing some distance from the front of Dole's Ash Farm, and then joining a track which meanders southwards between fields on an easy-going up and down. The going is good on a hard surface with nothing much around; when the track forks left and right (not very obvious) take the right fork, and continue down by the side of the woodland of Dole's Hill Plantation.

13. There's a bit of a quandary here. The main track continues straight ahead, and brings you out on the B3142 a couple of miles outside Puddletown. If the map is to be believed that's the way to go; I took the more direct easterly route, which posed some problems.

Firstly, it's not signposted and it's difficult to find the two turnings. Secondly, the first part takes you along the side of a field where there's no semblance of a track, and then on along a bumpy hillside which is equally hard going. After what seems like a long time but is in fact a short distance, you reach the main track, which is well overgrown with stinging nettles in high summer. This brings you down to Druce Farm; it's a little confusing here, but just keep on straight ahead and you'll hit the road, from where it's a five minute pedal into Puddletown.

Places To Visit:
Minterne Gardens on A352 north of Cerne Abbas
(tel: 01300 341370).

Top Pubs:
The Piddle Inn and The Poacher at Piddletrenthide;
The New Inn at Cerne Abbas.

Buckland Newton to Piddletrenthide

**Offroad and
On-Road**

Ride Area: West Dorset, due north of
Dorchester on the B3143.

OS Map: Landranger 194 – Dorchester,
Weymouth and surrounding area.

Route:
Piddletrenthide (GR:703000)
Kingcombe (GR:740002)
Nettlecombe Farm (GR:745015)
Folly (GR:728032)
Plush (GR:713021)
Buckland Newton (GR:688050)
Little Minterne Hill (GR:673040)
Higher Southcombe Farm (GR:681009)
Piddletrenthide (GR:703000)

Nearest BR Station: Maiden Newton/
Dorchester.

Approx Length: 18 miles (29km).

Time: Allow 3 hours.

Rating: Moderate. Some of the tracks
are quite hard going; care needs to be
taken with navigation.

Places To Visit:
Minterne Gardens (tel: 01300 341370)
at Minterne Magna (off route);
The Cerne Abbas Giant (off route).

Top Pubs:
The Brace of Pheasants at Plush;
The Gaggle of Geese at Buckland Newton;
The Poacher Inn at Piddletrenthide.

*This is a short classic with some fine views,
a fine pub, and some challenging tracks
with plenty of variety packed into its length.
The ride can be started from Piddletrenthide or Buckland Newton, both of
which are on the B3143.*

1. I chose to start from Piddletrenthide which
is that much closer to the county capital of
Dorchester. Opposite the Manor House at the
northern end of the village, take the road which
heads due east signposted to Cheselbourne.
Follow this uphill and out into the countryside,
passing Thorncombe Farm and then taking the
next left turn off the road at a bridleway crossing
signposted for Nettlecombe Farm.

2. Past the farm the tarmac lane becomes a
track, and it's a fine ride on a steady uphill along
the top of the down above Hog Hill. Keep
straight on northwards with the track, but when
you come to a solitary, rusty water tank in the
middle of a field, turn 90 degrees left as indicated
by the blue bridleway arrows.

3. This leads you into a belt of trees and
through a narrow bridleway gate, emerging on
the hillside above Lyscombe Bottom which is a
magical place with a huge, round bowl laid out
before you. Ride on along the top of Lyscombe
Hill by the side of the trees, looking for the first
big gate on the right. If you overshoot the track
ahead looks inviting, but swings south back down
to Thorncombe Farm.

4. Turn through the gate on the top of
Lyscombe Hill and you'll find another big view
on the other side. The bridleway arrows on this
gate are confusing, and the correct route heads
across a big field and down the hillside in a
north-north-west direction, joining a hard track
in the far corner at the bottom.

5. This track leads down to the road at Folly,
where you turn left to ride on to the hamlet of
Plush which is as smart as its name and boasts a
very pleasant pub in the Brace of Pheasants,

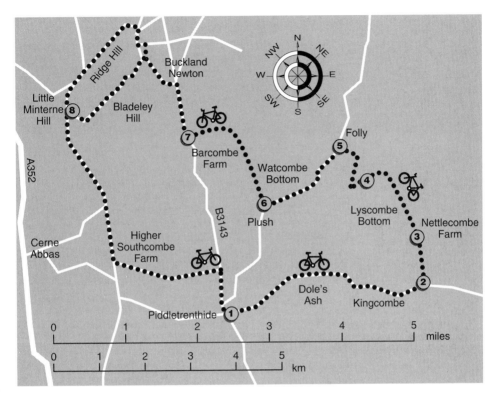

whose owner is a keen biker. Follow the road southwards past the pub, and a short way on take the first track on the right which heads up the hillside.

6. This track bears round to the right, emerging on the hilltop above Watcombe Bottom with more fine views laid out below. The signposting is quite good here as the main bridleway carries on along the top of the down, before turning left by the side of Church Hill to join a track which heads downhill to a solitary barn. The track carries on down the hillside to join the B3143 in the valley, though the bridleway bears off to the right before hitting the B3143 a short way to the north.

7. Turn right along the B3143, and after about a mile take the first lane on the left by a phone box which leads straight to Buckland Newton. Past the pub bear left if you want to follow the

track which leads up Bladeley Hill. To find it ride straight ahead through the farm entrance, and then turn right at the bridleway signposts.

Be warned that the lower section of this track can be atrociously muddy, and if it's been very wet you'd do better following the roads round the side of Ridge Hill.

8. At the top of Bladeley Hill turn left along the road above Little Minterne Hill to head due south. This is fast road-riding on a steady downhill past Giants Head, with Cerne Abbas in the valley below. Before the second turning for Cerne Abbas look out for the bridleway track that leads eastwards past Higher Southcombe Farm. This is a very good track, giving a fast, downhill ride all the way to Piddletrenthide, though it gets pretty bouncy near the bottom. When you hit the B3143 once again, turn right past The Poacher Inn and ride into the village.

Blandford Forest

**Offroad and
On-Road**

Area: West of Blandford Forum.

OS Map: Landranger 194 – Dorchester,
Weymouth and surrounding area.

Route:
Blandford Forum (GR:884062)
Old Warren Plantation (GR:870056)
Broadley Wood (GR:851063)
Turnworth Down (GR:813093)
Shillingstone Hill (GR:835093)
Durweston (GR:858086)
Travellers' Rest (GR:844070)
Bryanston (GR:873062)
Blandford Forum (GR:884062)

Nearest BR Station: Poole.

Approx Length: 15 miles (25km).

Time: Allow 2–3 hours.

Rating: Easy. A few minor climbs and a
steady climb from Durweston; mainly
very good tracks, though some sections
could be muddy; take care to choose the
right tracks through Blandford Forest.

*The Blandford area is well endowed with
bridleways and is highly rated by offroad
bikers. The riding is easy because essen-
tially the tracks are good and well signposted by blue bridleway blobs, with not
much up and down and a lot of pleasant
woodland. If you've come by car the easi-
est starting point is the large car park by
the Information Centre beside the River
Stour. However waiting here is limited, so
if you plan diversions and pub stops it's
better to leave your car at the end of the
main street on the other side of the town.*

1.   From the Information Centre turn left and
ride over the River Stour, passing the entrance
to Bryanston School. A little further on you
pass a right hand turning signposted 'Bryanston
^{1}/$_4$ mile'; go past this and take the next right-
hand fork, which is signposted to Winterborne
Stickland. Ride up an easy hill with farm buildings on the right, and just past the last building
turn right down the main driveway to the farm
by a bridleway sign, passing a line-up of beautifully painted old ploughs.

2.   The drive becomes a farm track, going
through a gate and heading towards trees at Old
Warren Plantation with fields on either side.
   Just before the trees you go through a gate
and then follow the narrow track that goes
round the left side of the plantation, heading
down to another gate. Go through and head
straight across grass towards more trees ahead,
with a farmhouse and a large old barn down in
the valley to the right. Go into the trees through
a gate, and follow the woodland track ahead
ignoring all crossing tracks. You eventually
come out of the trees at another gate, and head
across open grassland to the next gate with
houses at 'Kennels' ahead.

3.   Go through a gate by the fairly modern
house, joining a track and bearing right over a
cattle grid past a large farmstead to the right.
   Take the next 90-degree right turning
down a tarmac lane which soon brings you past

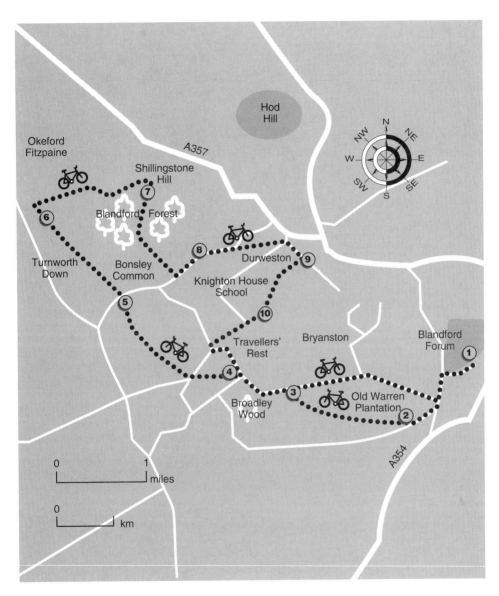

a few houses to the road. Turn left here, and follow this fairly quiet country road past Broadley Wood on your left. Ignore a right-hand fork, and a little further on where the road bends left with open fields and a gate ahead look for the bridleway sign which is on the

right-hand side pointing along the edge of the field.

4. Ride along this narrow track which bears left round the edge of the woods, and does not go straight across the field as shown on the OS map – a compromise which is better for both farmer and biker/horserider/walker. The track heads into the woods on a good surface, coming to a left and right fork marked by the familiar bridleway blobs.

Take the right fork here, and continue to follow your nose straight ahead through the woods at Field Grove, ignoring all side turnings as you ride along.

ahead across the right hand side of the field here, following the track past the next woods until you come to a T-junction crossing track at Cross Dyke within earshot of the road.

6. Turn right, passing the Forestry Commission sign for Wareham Forest. (If you want to head for the pub at Okeford Fitzpaine, turn left along the edge of the woods and take

Some bridleways in the Dorset countryside are well signposted and follow good tracks; others are not so bike friendly.

5. You eventually come out of the woods, passing through a gate and riding along the edge of a field with Blandford Forest ahead. Go ahead over a crossing track which is the bridleway leading down to the road from Shepherd's Corner Farm, and on along a much rougher track which is slow going and could be heavy riding in wet weather. Follow this track into the woods, keeping left on a better surface which runs along the woods' perimeter, coming out into the open at Turnworth Down. Keep on

the second bridleway turning which bears left over to the road, and then heads up towards Okeford Fitzpaine.)

Go into the woods on a fast forestry track which soon bears left with open ground on your right. After a while the track splits, with the right hand fork going past a trig point which is easily spotted. Keep to the main left-hand track here and follow it on a gradual descent through the woods along Shillingstone Hill – watch out for the deer which have a habit of darting across the track. Keep to the main track until you come to a right hairpin bend turning which is the way you go. This is easily spotted – the track sweeps round to the right uphill almost doubling back on itself, while straight ahead there is the start of a steep downhill with trees on either side. The latter track leads down to the road below Hod Hill where there are no connecting bridleways.

7. Follow the track round to the right and into the open with fields on either side. Pass a bridleway sign to the right, following the sign straight on and going once more into the woods ahead on a slight downhill. Here you take the right-hand fork along the good, wide track through the woods which bears left around Bonsley Common, passing a couple of huts on the left on the way. Go through a gate and follow the track across open ground towards more woods, going through a gate and riding along the left side of the trees until you reach the minor road ahead.

8. Turn left here past a few houses, the last one of which is called 'The Folly'. A little further downhill past a large barn, turn right through a five-bar metal gate with a bridleway sign. Head straight on down towards the trees ahead on a fast grass descent, looking for the gate at the bottom of the hill which soon comes into view.

Once through the gate keep to the right-hand track along the edge of trees, following it on a narrow woodland trail, and then through a narrow gate with a large field up to the left. This soon brings you down to a gate by a small equestrian centre. Ride straight through past the stables, and join the road in the petite village of Durweston.

9. Turn right along the road, right again, then immediately left passing the church. Keep on along this road past the houses, until you see a footpath sign showing the way ahead to Bryanston ('1 mile') along a long avenue of trees. Just to the right a bridleway sign points straight up the hill, a route which does not quite agree with the OS map. Head up here, and go through a gate at the top of the field with Knighton House School on your right. Turn right along a faint track above the school, and go through a gate and onto a rough crossing track.

10. Turn left uphill here, gradually heading up to Websley Farm, bearing left and right between the farmhouse and stables.

From here on follow the track straight ahead and down to the road opposite the farm at Travellers' Rest where there are a few choice buildings. Turn left along the road, bearing left uphill and following it past Broadley Wood. From here you can keep along this road which will take you down past Bryanston to Blandford; or if you prefer to return offroad, retrace the outward bridleway route which is mainly downhill and consequently more fun than on the way out, and you're soon back in Blandford after two to three hours in the saddle.

Places To Visit:
Blandford Forum Museum, Blandford Forum
(tel: 01258 454270).

Top Pubs:
The Royal Oak at Okeford Fitzpaine; pubs, cafes, etc in Blandford Forum.

Wareham Forest Circuit

*This is an on– and offroad cruise which
can be as demanding on technical ability
as you choose to make it, with some good
views and plenty of variety. There is no
hard climbing, but some of the going
through forestry is tricky – count the number of times you put a foot down, and then
add up your score at the end! You can
either start the ride from the centre of
Wareham, which is a pleasant old town
worth investigating; or else from the
Forestry Commission car park at the
southern end of the Wareham Forest.*

1. Head north-west out of Wareham on the
Bere Regis road. When you come into the forest, the Forestry Commission car park is on the
right about a mile out of town. From here carry
on along the road for just under another mile.
For the first hundred yards or so you can ride
offroad along the right side of the road; then
join the road and head on past the Silent
Woman and a caravan park on the left. A little
further on the bridleway joins the road from the
left. Cross the road and the bridleway goes
through a gate.

2. Head up this bridleway, keeping due north
all the way to Bloxworth. At first it goes down a
narrow track hemmed in by a wire fence with
open ground on the right. This section is surprisingly tricky due to the narrowness of the
track and bumps and lumps of tree roots under
your wheels – watch out also for the stream
which suddenly cuts a great trench across your
path.

3. Head on into Wareham Forest where the
track gets a great deal better. Keep straight
ahead through forest and open land, past
Woolbarrow Fort on your left. Wherever the
track deviates there are clear blue bridleway
blobs to guide you on your way, until eventually
you ride through a stream and come out onto
the A35, which links Bournemouth and Bere
Regis. Watch out when crossing!

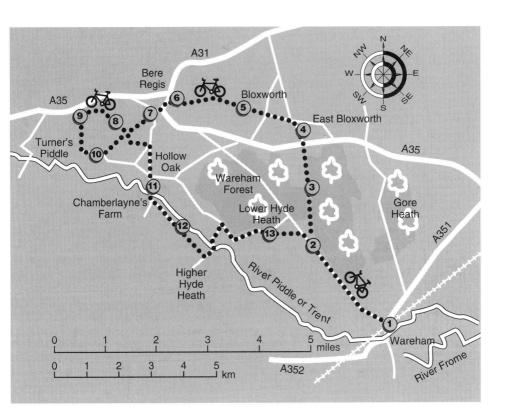

4. Go straight across here and keep ahead on a track which bends left past some houses, and then right taking you out onto the Bloxworth Road at East Bloxworth. Turn left for about three-quarters of a mile of quiet on-roading past the few sleepy houses of Bloxworth with fine views of the Dorset countryside away to your right. Keep on ahead at the dead-end road sign, past a building with a brewery sign sited next to the church. Pass a few modern bungalows, and then go through the gate ahead with a bridleway sign pointing straight across the field. To your right is Bloxworth House, a magnificent Jacobean pile hidden by trees.

5. The next gate is set in the perimeter of the woods on the far side of the field. At first sight these fields are welcoming with plenty of blue-bells in the spring, and there's a rusty sign which tells you that a 'Boundary Oak' was planted here to replace the one believed to have been there since the Domesday Book – the modern replacement didn't seem to be in evidence, however. From here the track degenerates due to being badly chewed up by tractors. After wet weather much of this short section is barely ridable. You soon cross a track where the bridleway greatly improves, becoming grassy and hard under your wheels with trees and rhododenderons on either side. Where the track forks, go left uphill as indicated by the blue bridleway blob; this is the first uphill of the ride and is short and easy.

6. You then continue west along a fine open section with good views to the north and to the south where you may see the vague outlines of the Atomic Energy Establishment at Winfrith.

Pause for a rest, check the map, make sure you know where you are and where you are going, then ride on.

The track enters trees and then goes through a gate by farm buildings, over a track, and through another gate. Head on down the track which bears right and left, coming to a twin bar gate which takes you across a field that goes steeply downhill with views of Bere Regis beyond. Head diagonally across this field following the horse tracks, and there's a good 'bike extreme' downhill in the bottom left corner leading down to a gate by a house from where a short track leads down to the road.

7. Turn right down this road past the farm and join the busy A31. Turn left for a short distance along it, turning right into Bere Regis at the roundabout. Follow the road round to the left, stopping if you like to look at the church, which is advertised as 'Medieval with an inter-

esting carved roof'. The road crosses the river, and immediately after you take the turning to the right for Southbrook, following it round to the left past a footpath sign until you see the cemetary ahead of you. The bridleway track goes up the right hand side of the cem-etery on a good surface, heading into trees.

8. Bridleway blobs indicate left and straight ahead. Take the straight ahead which goes up a short, steep hill and off to the right and onto open heath heading south-west. After a while you come to a crossing track where you turn right, heading north-west across the heath.

Ignore a track doubling back to the left (marked 'Tumuli' on the OS map), and keep straight on until you reach a gate with bridleways indicated downhill to the left and straight ahead towards some modern farm buildings. Keep on for the farm buildings, and when you reach them turn left through a gate following a bridleway blob. The track which goes straight ahead looks fast and inviting but is the wrong way! Instead bear right across the field (south-west), and into trees where you'll find a bridle-way gate.

9. Head on down a good fast track through Piddle Wood. When you pass an old shack on the left the track dips down to a crossroads where you turn left, heading on downhill in a southerly direction, and eventually breaking into open country.

After a good, fast descent turn left when you reach the crossing track and head east for Turner's Piddle, a small hamlet with a few houses, an attractive church, and a farm.

10. Just past the last barn the bridleway goes up to the left, heading up Damer Hill to Black Hill. This is the hardest uphill of the ride, but would be rated Moderate at worst. After going up through trees the track breaks into open ground where you come to a crossroads with a large unusual rock. Carry on to the next cross-roads at the top of Black Hill – where you turned right on the way out – and this time turn right in the other direction, along past the quar-ry, before bearing left on a good downhill via Hundred Barrow past a caravan park.

11. Here you join the road. Cross over and turn right for Wool, ignoring the turning to Bere Heath. After about a mile you cross the River Piddle at Chamberlayne's Bridge, and then bear left onto a track with a faded bridle-way blob before you reach the pylons.

Head along this track past farm and other buildings, crossing a stream and going into rhododenderon woods. These woods are very pretty despite a few mini dumps of building materials, and the route of the bridleway is clearly marked. Eventually you emerge on the right-hand side of a square clearing. Keep straight ahead, and then go through a lumber

yard and out onto the road via a gate opposite Newfoundland.

12. Turn left along this minor road which snakes its way across the Piddle and its off-shoots, past a house on the left named Woodlands, before bending left, running straight, and then bending left again when the forest comes into view with pylons beyond.

Bere Lodge is a small white building on the right side of this bend with the bridleway run-ning beside it – first time it's easily missed. Turn down the bridleway heading SSE on a good track with woods to your left and open ground to the right. When you come to a cross-roads turn left as indicated by a bridleway blob. The track continues on a hard gravel surface, with rhododenderons on either side, which must be magnificent when in flower.

13. After about half a mile turn right off this track and into woods, as indicated by two bri-dleway blobs. On my visit the woods here had been decimated by the foresters, but the area may have been properly cleared by the time you get to it. Follow the bridleway through to open heathland where there's a conspicuous rock with faded footpath and bridleway blobs. Follow the bridleway direction which is straight ahead and due east, taking you out onto the road just above North Trigon Farm. Here you turn right to ride back along the road towards Wareham some three miles away.

Places To Visit:
Bovington Tank Museum
(tel: 01929 463953).

Top Pubs:
The Silent Woman at Cold Harbour two miles north-west of Wareham.

Winterborne Tour

**Offroad and
On-Road**

Ride Area: East Dorset, between Bere Regis and Blandford Forum.

OS Map: Landranger 194 – Dorchester, Weymouth and surrounding area.

Route:
Winterborne Kingston (GR:862977)
Charlton Down (GR:875008)
Thornicombe Farm (GR:855028)
Winterborne Clenston (GR:840030)
Hewish Farm (GR:805003)
Milborne St Andrew (GR:802976)
Winterborne Kingston (GR:862977)

Nearest BR Station: Poole.

Approx Length: 19 miles (30km).

Time: Allow 3 hours.

Rating: Moderate. Riding difficulties will depend on conditions; bridleway signposting is poor.

This is a bracing circuit of Dorset countryside inland, where there are plenty of bridleways though they're not always clearly marked or easily passable. There are some good views from high ground along the way, and although you could start from anywhere on the circuit we opted for Winterborne Kingston.

1. From Winterborne Kingston, ride round the back of the church to East Street where you head east. Beyond the houses the lane becomes a track which comes to farm buildings at Abbot's Court on the left. Here the main track goes through a gate and curves round to the left, but you keep to the right and head straight along the side of the field ahead.

Follow this good track on to the next field where you meet a track coming up from a farm to the right. This goes ahead for a short distance and then turns 90 degrees to the left, at which point you go straight ahead on a narrow track running along the left-hand side of a hedge. Keep on in the same direction, following the track across the open field beyond, and coming to a gate where you drop down onto a gravelled crossing track.

2. Turn left here, and follow the track which passes farm buildings on the left at Goschen, bears right and left, and then after about a mile becomes a grass track heading straight into the woods. Go into these woods which are on the top of Charlton Down, and turn left on the first crossing track which takes you out to the west side. Here you turn left on a narrow track running along the side of the wire boundary fence, soon coming to a gate where you leave the woods. Ignore the turning to the left and head across to a narrow track going straight ahead into the bushes. This was fairly overgrown but ridable when I tackled it, heading downhill.

After a time you will meet a wide track coming from the left; turn left along it, keeping left until you see a couple of posts with a blue bridleway mark ahead. Go through here, and ride on downhill by the side of a battery egg

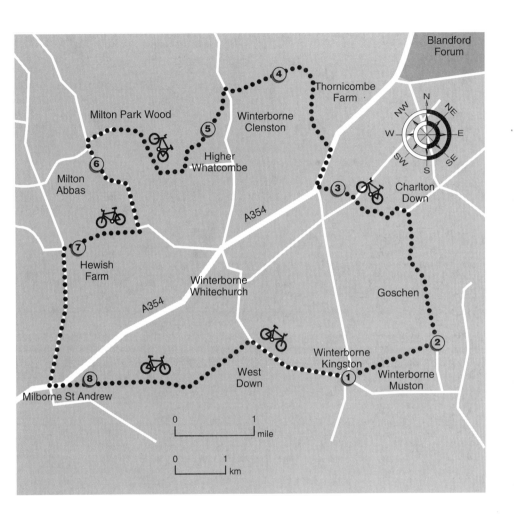

Blandford
Forum

Milton Park Wood

Winterborne
Clenston

Thornicombe
Farm

Higher
Whatcombe

Milton
Abbas

Charlton
Down

A354

Hewish
Farm

Winterborne
Whitechurch

Goschen

A354

Winterborne
Kingston

West
Down

Winterborne
Muston

Milborne St Andrew

0   1
|_____| mile

0   1
|_____| km

farm, joining the tarmac driveway and eventually coming out at the road past a yellow road barrier by a sign for East Down House – a bridleway sign pointing back the way you came confirms that this is the right way!

3. Turn right along the road which leads to the busy A354 after fifty yards. Turn right, and ride along past a driveway going down to the farmstead at Whatcombe Down on the left.

A few hundred yards further on a footpath sign on the left points up a track going uphill to the right. You turn left on to the bridleway here, heading north across the field on what was a good, clear track when I rode it. At the far side of the field you go through a gate and join a narrow track between a hedge and wire fence running up the side of the field ahead. Keep on going until you come to a gate at the end, and there bear left into a field which goes down and uphill ahead of you. There is no indication of where you should ride, but since the bridleway gate is in the far right-hand corner it seems sensible to keep to the right side of the field.

89

4. Go through the gate and continue to ride along the side of the field, coming out by the side of an electricity pylon where you cross underneath the power-lines by riding down the left side of the field ahead. When you start to head uphill, look for a narrow track through the hedge on the left. This takes you to a gate, where you head straight across the left side of the field ahead with a pylon on your right. You soon join a rough track which bears left and right, taking you down past the large farmstead at Winterborne Clenston, and then steeply downhill to the road by an impressive old barn.

5. Turn right along the road here, passing the front of the Manor House. Well before the phone box a bridleway track going up to the left is indicated, passing through a locked green gate – it appears that horses are expected to squeeze round the side.

Follow the tarmac track uphill as it bears round to the left and into thick woods. It goes past an incongruously placed garage on level ground, and from there straight on past another gate to a narrow, overgrown track through Oatclose Wood. This leads to an old gate where you turn on to a better track that bears left through the woods, eventually bringing you into the open by another gate. Turn right inside the fence here, and head steeply downhill by the side of the woods with the clearing of Higher Whatcombe to your left. At the bottom go through a gate and turn left on a crossing track, riding to the south-west corner of the clearing where you turn right on a wide Forestry Track by the Wareham Forest sign.

6. Follow this track as it bears north through Milton Park Wood, heading west past a solitary cottage after which it emerges on the road just outside Milton Abbas – a fine looking village with a famous school and agreeable pub. From there follow the road south past the trig point on the side of Hoggen Down, going past Luccombe Farms on the right.

7. About half a mile further on the road

bends left. The track off to the right is the bridleway, following the right-hand side of the field and then turning left along the bottom where it comes to a gate. Turn right through this gate, and go straight ahead along the right side of the next field until you come to a gate in the far right corner. Here you turn right and left along the perimeter of another field, joining a track which passes a modern barn on the left and soon brings you down to the road by Hewish Farm next to a field with geese.

8. Turn left along the road here, and ride on for about one and a half miles into Milborne St Andrew. At the main road – the pub is a short way to the right – turn left and then first right, following a quiet lane straight on and round to the left where it goes uphill past houses. At the crossroads turn left, and then look for a gate on the right with a faded blue bridleway arrow.

Turn right here, heading eastwards along the left side of the hedge across farmland. Go through the next gate, and in the field beyond go through the gate on the right so that you follow the hedge on your left, keeping in the same direction. The bridleway passes a cottage on the right, heading downhill and uphill, following the line of hedges on the left. Eventually it comes to the road by West Down where you turn right to ride for just over one mile into Winterborne Kingston. Alternatively you can follow the bridleway past Bere Down which leads straight to the village

---

Places to Visit:
Milton Park Farm Museum near Milton Abbas (tel: 01258 880704);
Tolpuddle Martyrs Museum at Tolpudde to the south-west of Milborne St Andrew (tel: 01305 848237).

Top Pubs:
The Greyhound Inn at Winterborne Kingston;
The Hambro Arms at Milton Abbas.

Badbury Rings Ride

Mainly Offroad

Ride Area: East Dorset, to the north-west of Wimborne Minster.

OS Map: Landranger 195 – Bournemouth, Purbeck and surrounding area.

Route:
Badbury Rings CP (GR:961032)
Witchampton (GR:987063)
Tarrant Monkton (GR:945091)
Abbeycroft Down (GR:950053)
Tarrant Crawford (GR:923027)
Shapwick (GR:943020)
Kingston Lacy (GR:972010)
King Down Farm (GR:970038)
Badbury Rings (GR:961032)

Nearest BR Station: Poole.

Approx Length: 20 miles (32km).

Time: Allow 3 hours.

Rating: Moderate. Mainly easy riding, but there's a lot of offroad work. Could be muddy in wet weather.

This is an excellent ride through fine countryside, within easy reach of Poole or Bournemouth. The tracks here are at their best in early summer; at other times there could be some muddy going. Badbury Rings makes a good place to start from, with a free car park close to the iron age fort that takes its name; otherwise you can connect with this ride by road and bridleway from Wimborne Minster.

1. From the Badbury Rings car park follow the bridleway sign straight ahead to the northeast past the horseshoe shaped track, going downhill through a gate and then up into woods by King Down Farm. From here the bridleway continues in much the same direction, joining a narrow track between high hedges which can be very overgrown in summer – plenty of nettles and all kind of wild flowers – but which remains ridable as it eventually brings you to the road between Hemsworth and Bradford Farm.

2. Go straight ahead here, following the quiet road towards Witchampton by the side of the River Allen, and taking the second left turn that heads to the north-west. Just past a very fancy barn conversion on the left, you'll come to a bridleway track on the right; take this to continue northwards to the next road junction, where there's a wonderful old Victorian schoolhouse just as you hit the road. (If you want to link straight on to Ride 22, go straight ahead here following the dead straight Roman Road bridleway to join the road between Gussage St Michael and Gussage All Saints).

3. Take a left by the phone box, riding westwards towards Manswood where you turn right to continue north, bearing left onto the next bridleway track which heads west across the north side of Chetterwood.

This is a wide, fast track which is easy riding, leading to the hillside above Tarrant Monkton where you have the choice of following the bridleway as it swings round to the south, or bearing right onto a track by a gate

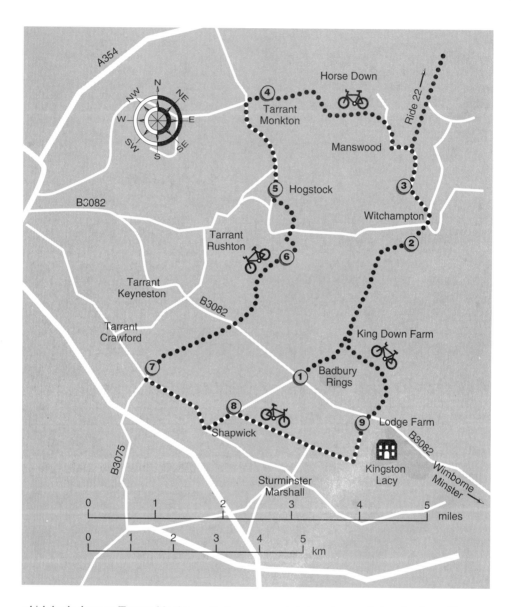

which leads down to Tarrant Monkton with its watersplash and pleasantly sited pub.

4. If you go down into Tarrant Monkton, follow the back road south from the pub, crossing the River Tarrant by Manor Farm and rejoining the road that leads to Tarrant Rushton. Follow the road until it bends fairly sharply to the right by the side of The Cliff; here you'll find a track that goes straight ahead up the hillside, rejoining the bridleway that continues due south.

5. A short way on the bridleway becomes a made-up road. Before you reach the first houses at Hogstock, follow the alternative road which bears left (south-east), heading down through the woods to join the road just opposite the old Tarrant Rushton airfield. Cross the road and you'll find a track that leads on to the north-east corner of the runways.

6. It's a strange sensation cycling on a disused airfield, and it's a perfect place for practice if you're into time trialling. Follow the eastern arm southwards, taking a right and a left turn at a junction (the bridleway signs are a little confusing here) to head south-west to the road about one mile east of Tarrant Rushton.

You'll find a locked gate at the road; the bridleway actually follows the side of the main track but is extremely overgrown, and happily there is no problem getting through the gate with a bike.

7. Over the road the track goes straight ahead in the same south-west direction, following the side of fields where it can be overgrown but still ridable. Keep on straight ahead (or divert if you want to visit Tarrant Crawford), turning left at the road and following it into Shapwick by the side of the River Stour.

8. Turn left by the pub at Shapwick, and then take the next right turn past New Barn Farm, crossing the next road to join a bridleway track which heads across flat country to the south-west corner of the grounds of Kingston Lacy.

Where the bridleway splits left and right, take the left fork to the B3082 road by Lodge Farm – if you want to visit Kingston Lacy, the entrance is a short way along the road to the east from here.

9. Cross straight over the B3082, turn right, and a very short way on take the first bridleway track to the left past Lodge Farm which leads northwards on a good fast surface. When you come to an isolated barn, take the left turning bridleway and follow it west towards King

Down Farm, riding uphill into the woods and joining the outward track where you turn left (south) for the Badbury Rings car park.

Turning for home by the Anchor Inn at Shapwick, close to Kingston Lacy.

Places To Visit:
Kingston Lacy House NT
(tel: 01202 883402);
Badbury Rings iron age hill fort.

Top Pubs:
The Langton Arms at Tarrant Monkton;
The Anchor Inn at Shapwick.

Cranborne Chase

Offroad and On-Road

Ride Area: East Dorset, near the Wiltshire border.

OS Maps: Landrangers 195/184 – Bournemouth, Purbeck and surrounding area/Salisbury and The Plain.

Route:
Cranborne (GR:055133)
Sixpenny Handley (GR:995173)
Tollard Royal (GR:943178)
Ashmore (GR:913180)
Tarrant Gunville (GR:924130)
Chettle (GR:950133)
Gussage St Michael (GR:986115)
Gussage All Saints (GR:003106)
Wimborne St Giles (GR:030120)
Cranborne (GR:055133)

Nearest BR Station: Tisbury.

Approx Length: 34 miles (55km).

Time: Allow 4–5 hours.

Rating: Moderate. The tracks are good and there is no serious hill climbing, but it's a fair distance.

This is a great ride in the north-east corner of Dorset, exploring some beautiful countryside close to the Wiltshire border and visiting a series of attractive small villages along the way. Cranborne on the B3078 to the north-west of Ringwood makes a good place to start, but you could as easily choose anywhere on the circuit.

1. From the centre of Cranborne turn west past the fine church, following the minor road which leads northwards. Take the first fork on the left, and join a bridleway which heads up towards Toby's Bottom, leaving the tarmac as it becomes a good track all the way across Blackbush Down. This section is mainly uphill riding, but when you reach a gate by the side of woodland at Pentridge you have your reward as it's downhill on the other side, with great views ahead over Penbury Knoll.

2. At the bottom of the hill turn left to join a good track which heads westwards past the woodland at Long Barrow. (The track which continues north leads to the village of Pentridge). Take the right hand fork, and follow the narrow track ahead to the A354 by the side of a garage.

3. Cross straight over the A354, following the bridleway round the side of a field by Oakley's Down which is quite hard riding. The bridleway then leads downhill between two fields by Wor Barrow, eventually joining a lane to come out on the road a short distance to the north of Sixpenny Handley – one of those villages that has 'grown', with a lot of modern additions springing up.

4. Ride into Sixpenny Handley, turning right at the crossroads to follow the B3081 westwards for three miles or so on to Tollard Royal.

This is pleasant enough riding – though rather less pleasant if there's a strong west wind – with a long downhill by the side of Minchington Down, crossing into Wiltshire where Tollard Royal is a lovely little place with a small

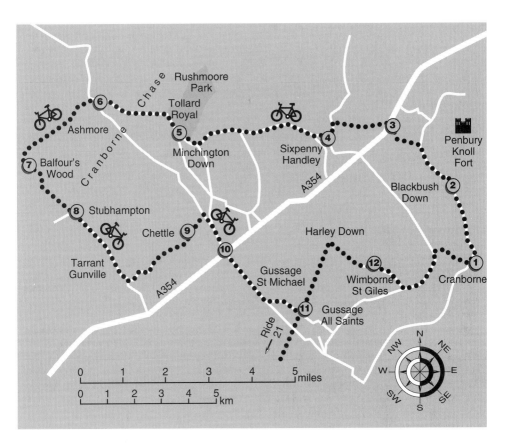

pond by the roadside (great for a picnic) and the King John pub nearby. The village takes its name from King John's hunting lodge which dates from the thirteenth century.

5. From Tollard Royal the route continues westwards along the B3081 which climbs fairly steeply up the side of Woodley Down with fine views opening out to the north over Berwick St John. There is an optional bridleway route here. It starts just past the pub by the side of a rather smart converted chapel, heading up the hillside and bearing right round the back of the house at the top, but at this stage of the ride there's still some way to go and the road option is quicker.

6. At the top of Woodley Down the road

bears round to the north. On this bend take the left turn onto a minor road which brings you back into Dorset, almost immediately turning right into Ashmore. Follow the road south-west out of Ashmore, ignoring the first bridleway you come to on the left and heading steeply downhill to Washers Pit.

7. When you reach Balfour's Wood at the bottom of the hill, turn left onto the hard gravel forestry track and follow it into the woodland, ignoring the other bridleway which is signposted back up the hill. The track winds south-east through Southampton Bottom and is at first really good riding. Further on the going gets more difficult and could be muddy; it's also easy to stray off the bridleway which bears right

The long descent from the top of Blackbush Down, with more than thirty miles of good riding still ahead.

down the hillside, following the valley bottom on a narrow track in the same south-easterly direction, and eventually leaving the woods and emerging on the road by a few houses at the bottom of Stubhampton Down.

8. Follow the road straight ahead through Stubhampton, and on to Tarrant Gunville where you'll find the Bugle Horn Inn beyond the village on the right side of the road.

Take the next left turning onto a dead-end lane by the corner of Eastbury House, following this lane north-east onto a byway track which in summer becomes severely overgrown and is certainly impassable by vehicles. Keep on straight ahead by the side of a water tower, following the track between fields and into trees on the outskirts of Chettle where the byway crosses open parkland by Chettle House before coming to the road.

9. At Chettle turn left and then take the first bridleway on the right. This continues north-east across fields on a steady uphill and with no proper track is heavy going; in wet weather it could be dismal, and an alternate road-route is recommended. Turn right at the next lane and follow it south-east, joining another lane which brings you to the A354 by the side of Week Street Down.

10. Cross over the A354, following the road south-east and then taking the first left turn downhill into Gussage St Michael. Bear right with the road past the church here, continuing south-east towards Gussage All Saints where you may care to pay a visit to the well-known Drovers Arms.

11. About halfway between Gussage St Michael and Gussage All Saints a bridleway track heads north-east between the fields, starting by the side of water board premises where it connects with Ride 21. Follow this track on a dead straight Roman Road to the woodland at Harley Down, turning right at a clearly signposted bridleway crossroads to follow a fast,

Ashmore with its fine pond is one of many picturesque places along this route, which has something of everything.

hard track south-east towards Wimborne St Giles – it's fast, easy riding in very pleasant surroundings here.

12. Follow the road into Wimborne St Giles which is a magical little place with a wonderful church. Ride along the road to the north-east, joining the B3081 for half a mile and then turning right and then left for Cranborne, with a very fine and fast downhill to complete this excellent ride.

Places To Visit:
Cranborne Manor Gardens
(tel: 01725 517248).

Top Pubs:
The King John at Tollard Royal;
The Bugle Horn at Tarrant Gunville;
The Drovers Arms at Gussage All Saints.

The New Forest

The New Forest is neither new or much of a forest. It has been there a long time, though most of the ancient trees have gone and are now replaced by areas of Forestry Commission 'Inclosures'. The result is a mixture of forest and open heath, with woodland that in the main avoids regimented lines of Forestry Commission conifers, and has a pleasing mixture of broad-leaf trees and some very attractive areas.

The New Forest welcomes offroad cyclists, who are free to use all the main gravelled track forest roads, but are asked to keep off the secondary tracks and trails. These forest roads can provide very good riding and are particularly good for familes, but please remember that the New Forest is popular with walkers and horse riders, and stick by the New Forest Cycling Code:

● Give way to walkers and horse riders, particularly children. Travel at moderate speed and avoid bunching in a group.

● Always keep to made-up gravelled tracks in the woodland Inclosures and on the Open Forest.

● Please take care of the Forest. Avoid wheel spins and skidding. Erosion of tracks is a serious problem.

● Approach and pass Forest ponies and cattle with caution. They do not understand cyclists.

● Know where you are going and take a map and compass.

Ride 23: New Forest North Side

Ride 24: New Forest South Side

Ride 25: New Forest East Side

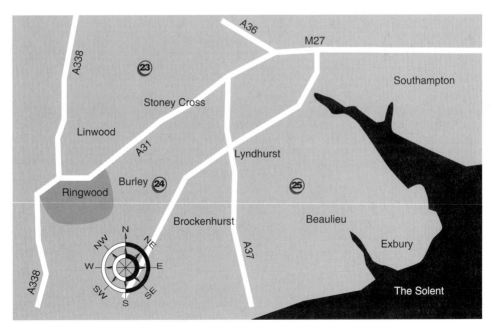

New Forest North Side

Ride Area: The New Forest, north of the A31.

OS Map: Landranger 195 – Bournemouth, Purbeck and surrounding area.

Route:
Linwood CP (GR:183093)
Bratley Plain Trig Point (GR:218089)
Ocknell Plain CP (GR:231121)
Coppice of Linwood (GR:247148)
Fritham (231142)
Hampton Ridge Trig Point (GR:185136)
Frogham (GR:172129)
Mockbeggar (GR:160093)
Linwood (GR:183093)

Nearest BR Station: Sway.

Approx Length: 22 miles (35km).

Time: Allow 3 hours.

Rating: Easy. There are few hills, the tracks are very good, and the navigation is mainly straightforward.

This ride is an excellent introduction to the New Forest, which is at its best on the north side of the A31 where there are comparatively few settlements and some of the mystery of the New Forest still remains. Most of the distance is offroad and is very good riding, while on-road you will have the pleasure of seeing cars restricted to 40mph.

1. There are a number of forest car parks round the route, and the one on the outskirts of Linwood makes a good start point. Ride past the pub and its attendant caravan site, and follow the road east. As the road bends round to the left fork right onto a hard forest road, and follow this through a gate into the woods, crossing Linford Brook and riding eastwards past King's Garden to the trig point on Bratley Plain close by the A31.

2. From the trig point follow the track round to the left, bearing right into woodland and crossing a road to ride on through Slufters Inclosure as the track bears north to join the road by Ocknell Plain – a very popular area with the local horses. Turn right onto the road here, and follow it in a north-east direction across Ocknell Plain to the T-junction at Janesmoor Plain. Here you can either turn left along the road and follow the signs to Fritham, or if you are in the mood for an extra offroad loop explore the forest roads that lead through King's Garn Gutter Inclosure and the Coppice of Linwood to the east.

3. For the extra loop turn right along the road and then almost immediately left, following the concrete track past a water tower and on through an extensive, but very tasteful, caravan site. It's all downhill here and high speeds are possible, but with caravan families and children around it makes sense to ride safely and sensibly and take it slow.

At the end of the caravan site the forest road bears left to head northwawrds through the woodland of King's Garn Gutter Inclosure. From here on you need to refer to the OS map

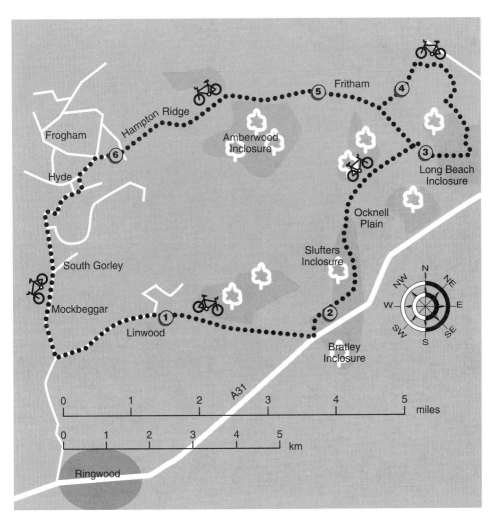

and a good sense of direction to keep on course. If all goes well you'll follow the side of the Coppice of Linwood on a winding uphill track by Salisbury Trench; the forest roads are all very good here, and if you find yourself on a road with a poor surface it means you've strayed off the route.

4. The forest road emerges from the woods by a radio mast where you join the road proper. Turn left here, and then bear right for Fritham, passing a strange 'tower house' on the corner and then dropping down into Fritham itself where the the Royal Oak is the friendly and unpretentious pub.

5. Keep straight on past the Royal Oak, riding into the woods signposted to the car park. Where the forest road splits, take the left fork which leads westwards. This is the start of a really good ride along Hiscocks Hill, through Amberwood Inclosure, and on to the Hampton

A typical scene on the north side of the Forest. The tracks here are excellent and it's open country so you won't lose the way.

Ridge trig point where the surroundings are as wild as the New Forest can be. It's relatively easy to find the way – just avoid right turn-offs, and follow the main track west and then south-west past the tumuli, eventually reaching the road at the bottom of a hill by Abbots Well.

6. At Abbots Well ride up the hill and into Frogham, passing the pub where you take the first left turn across Hyde Common to Hyde, a strange little place where you'll find donkeys

The Royal Oak makes a very pleasant place to stop, before the ride westwards across the open Forest.

strolling across the road. Turn left by the schoolhouse, and follow the narrow road south-west through Hungerford, dropping downhill to North Gorley from where the road heads due south to Mockbeggar. Further on the road crosses Dockens Water in a very pleasant set-ting – you'll often find an ice-cream van with kids splashing in the water here – and the next left turn heads back into the forest with Linwood a couple of miles further on.

> ***Places To Visit:***
> The Rufus Stone (GR:271123);
> New Forest Water Park
> (tel: 01425 656868);
> Paultons Park
> (tel: 01703 814455).
>
> ***Top Pubs:***
> The Royal Oak at Fritham;
> The Red Shoot at Linwood.

New Forest South Side

Mainly Offroad

Ride Area: The New Forest, south of the A31 on the Ringwood side.

OS Map: Landranger 195 – Bournemouth, Purbeck and surrounding area.

Route:
Burley (GR:211030)
Castle Hill (GR:199041)
Burley Street (GR:206043)
Mogshade Hill Cross (GR:240093)
Minstead (GR:281110)
Portuguese Fireplace (GR:265077)
Knightwood Inclosure (GR:256062)
Burley Lawn (GR:225031)
Burley (GR:211030)

Nearest BR Station: Sway.

Approx Length: 21 miles (34km).

Time: Allow 3 hours.

Rating: Easy/Moderate – there is a surprising amount of up and downing for the New Forest, some of the forest roads can be muddy, and care needs to be taken with navigation.

There are car parks all over the place on the south side of the New Forest, but Burley – which is a busy tourist centre – makes a good place to start this ride. If you can't stand the traffic which is pretty awful here in summer, try the Castle Hill car park about half a mile to the west of Burley Street; alternatively the Picket Post car park (GR:192060) would make an ideal start point for those coming off the A31.

1. From the centre of Burley bear left onto the Bransgore road. By the last houses look for Castle Lane on the right, and follow it northwards on a track that leads up to the Castle Hill fort, and then down to the road by the car park. Turn right here, and ride eastwards into the village of Burley Street.

2. Take the first left turn into Forest Road, following it across Burley Moor to join the main Burley Road. Turn left here, and where the road bends right by the side of forestry, go straight ahead through a gate to join a forest road that leads through South Oakley Inclosure.

3. From South Oakley Inclosure the forest track meanders in a north-east direction through Beech Bed Inclosure and North Oakley Inclosure on the way to the commemorative Cross by the roadside at Mogshade Hill. It's easy riding, but it can be muddy, care needs to be taken to stay on the main track, and you must ride slowly for walkers.

4. From the Cross at Mogshade Hill follow the forest road downhill into the Highland Wood Inclosure, crossing Highland Water by a bridge and taking the next left fork on a forest road that leads through Wick Wood. Go through the next gate, and follow the forest road past the car park by Acres Down House, riding on to the road on the outskirts of Newtown.

5. Cross straight over the road, and follow the narrow country lane ahead for a mile or so into

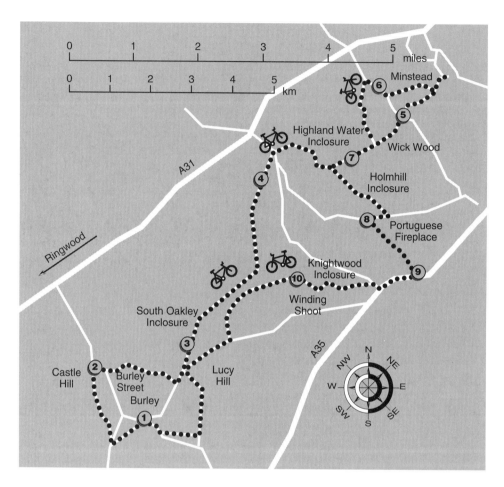

Minstead where the pub is in a fine setting by the village green, with a big seat round the tree in the middle and the local store's just opposite.

When you have exhausted Minstead retrace your tracks up the hill, taking the first right turn followed by a left turn to join a bridleway that runs east–west past a few houses to join the road below The Grove.

6. Follow the road to the north-west, passing a few posh houses with some unfriendly signs – 'Don't Attempt To Enter On Foot Or Our Dogs Will Get You' was one that stood out.

Look out for the first forest road on the

left, and follow this track along the edge of forestry at Withybed Bottom, bearing left to head south into the woods, heading steeply downhill by a lonely bench to rejoin the outward route at Wick Wood. Navigation around here requires some care.

7. From Wick Wood retrace your wheel tracks to the south-west. Ignore the first turning and take the second forestry road on the left, which will lead you in a south-east direction downhill through Holmhill Inclosure by the side of Highland Water, emerging on the road by a small car park/picnic site.

Minstead makes a convenient place for a rest. The pub is right opposite the village store.

8. Turn right here, and ride a short distance to check out the strange Portuguese Fireplace – a relic left by the Portuguese soldiers who were stationed in this unlikely place during the First World War. Just past the Fireplace take the first forest road on the left; follow it a short way south and then turn left on another forest road, riding south-east past the New Forest Reptiliary where you can see great pits of snakes from spring to autumn. From there it's a short distance to the A35.

9. Turn right along the A35 which is a beastly, busy road. It is possible to avoid the A35 if you keep south on the forest road from the Portuguese Fireplace. On the corner where it bears south-west, a track continues southwards to Knightwood Oak. This track can be gruesomely muddy, and in New Forest terms you should stick to the 'roads'.

Take the first right turn off the A35 and ride to the Knightwood Oak car park. Turn onto the forest road opposite – to start with it's quite rough and unkempt by New Forest standards – which heads south-west on a slight up-hill before turning right-left, and again right-left through the Knightwood Inclosure to Winding Shoot. You need to take care with the navigation here.

10. From Winding Shoot follow the forest road to the west, passing Anderwood Inclosure and Burley Outer Rails Inclosure before coming to the road half a mile north-east of Lucy Hill.

Turn right along the road which is dead straight and a steady downhill, taking the next left turning just before you cross your outward route, to head south past Burley Lawn. Ride over the next crossroads, turning right by the hotel on the corner to follow a track westwards past Cottesmore House, the YHA New Forest Hostel (tel: 01425 403233). This well-potholed track leads on to the cricket green on the outskirts of Burley. Turn right here, and follow the road downhill into the traffic hurley of Burley to complete the ride.

Places To Visit:

The New Forest Deer Sanctuary;
The New Forest Reptiliary. For more information contact the Forestry Commission (tel: 01703 283771).

New Forest East Side

Mainly Offroad

Ride Area: The eastern part of the New Forest, to the south-west of Southampton.

OS Map: Landranger 196 – Solent and the Isle of Wight.

Route:
Lyndhurst (GR:298081)
Clayhill (GR:301073)
Park Hill (GR:320060)
Denny Wood (GR:335059)
Frame Heath Inclosure (GR:347035)
Hawkhill Inclosure (GR:355026)
Hatchet Gate (GR:370018)
Beaulieu (GR:386020)
Hatchet Gate (GR:370018)
Hatchet Moor (GR:350002)
Round Hill (GR:333020)
Park Hill (GR:320060)
Clayhill (GR:301073)
Lyndhurst (GR:298081)

Nearest BR Station:
Brockenhurst/Beaulieu Road.

Approx Length: 20 miles (32km).

Time: Allow 3 hours.

Rating: Easy/Moderate. It's easy, flat riding, but there is a confusing mass of tracks and getting lost is easy.

The strange thing about the New Forest is that there's not much forest at all. The area to the immediate south-east of Lyndhurst has one of the densest wooded areas, which combined with forest tracks and lookalike forestry makes it easy to get lost in normal Forestry Commission style. It's important to pay careful attention to your compass and map – once you find the way, the riding is excellent and fast.

1. Lyndhurst is a very pleasant small town and the unofficial 'capital' of the New Forest area, though plagued by traffic which reaches its height on fine summer weekends when hordes of car-borne travellers attempt to find seclusion in the New Forest – it's much better by bike.

From Lyndhurst follow the main A337 southwards for half a mile or so; then opposite a phone box turn left up a lane between a thatched cottage and the farm animal breeding station at Clayhill. Ride on to the heavily reinforced gate (to keep out mad cows?), and enter the forest.

2. At the first the forest road is easy to follow as it heads south-east to Park Hill. It then enters a clearing where you turn right through a gate, and from there on great care needs to be taken with navigation if you are to find the way to the other side! Take the first or second forest road turning on the left – both lead to Denny Wood, though there are more wiggles than the OS map shows along the way.

3. Turn right at the forest road T-junction, and follow the main forest road south downhill past the small group of houses in a clearing at Denny Lodge, re-entering the forest at another gate and keeping due south to cross the railway by a bridge from the Perrywood Haseley Inclosure. Turn left onto the forest road that runs east parallel to the railway along Frame Heath Inclosure, and then take the next forest road turn to head south, turning east at the forest road crossroads to pass Moon Hill. Sounds

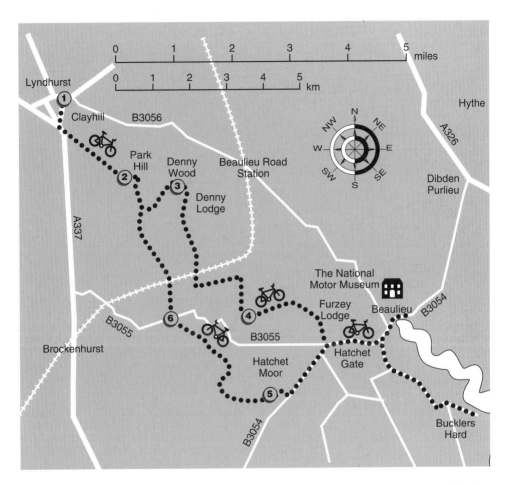

complicated? It is; you will surely get lost; but that's all part of the fun of riding here.

4. From Moon Hill the forest road bears right on a long downhill to a gate, coming out of the forestry and heading uphill across open ground to the hamlet of Furzey Lodge where there's a car park. Follow the road due south to the B3054 at Hatchet Gate, and if you wish to visit Beaulieu with its multiple attractions of Motor Museum, Palace House and old ruined Abbey, follow the B3054 east for a mile or so. You may also like to divert to Bucklers Hard on the Beaulieu River which is just over three miles to

the south-west, where the attractions include a maritime museum, historic cottage displays and a popular pub at the Master Builder Hotel.

5. To resume the ride, follow the B3054 south-west from Hatchet Gate, passing Hatchet Pond. After about a mile look out for the track that leads to the car park on the south side of Hatchet Moor; follow this track to the west and then round to the north-west, taking the first track on the left to join a concrete surface on this old airfield that heads north-east through a huge caravan/camp site, passing the pond at Round Hill and emerging on the B3055 by

The New Forest is famous for its horses and ponies. As with walkers, you should treat them with respect.

Perrywood Ironshill – once again navigation is confusing through here.

6. Cross straight over the B3055, joining a forest road which heads north past a few houses into New Copse Inclosure, before re-crossing the railway line and heading north through the forestry back to Park Hill – en route you'll find a confusion of tracks with good opportunities for getting lost. From Park Hill retrace your wheel tracks to Lyndhurst, where there are some pleasant tea houses to stop at if it's the right time of day.

Places To Visit:
New Forest Museum & Visitor Centre in Lyndhurst (tel: 01703 283914); Palace House, Beaulieu Church and Abbey Ruins, National Motor Museum at Beaulieu (tel: 01590 612345).

Top Pubs:
The Montagu Arms at Beaulieu; The Crown at Lyndhurst.

Cycling Books from the Crowood Press

Great Cycle Routes – North and South Downs	Jeremy Evans
Great Cycle Routes – Dartmoor and Exmoor	Jeremy Evans (July 1995)
50 Mountain Bike Rides	Jeremy Evans
Adventure Mountain Biking	Carlton Reid
Cycle Sport	Peter Konopka
Offroad Adventure Cycling	Jeremy Evans
Touring Bikes	Tony Oliver
Mountain Biking – The Skills of the Game	Paul Skilbeck